# *The* HUNGRY STUDENT
# Easy Baking

# *The* HUNGRY STUDENT
# *Easy Baking*

## Charlotte Pike

# CONTENTS

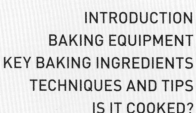

# INTRODUCTION

**Welcome to the first-ever baking book just for students!**

Believe it or not, the humble student kitchen is a great place to bake. It requires very little equipment, the main ingredients are seriously cheap, and you'll be the most popular housemate every time you whip up a batch of cookies or cupcakes. You may have a wonky oven or think you can't even break an egg properly, but whatever your level of experience, you will find plenty of great, easy treats to tempt you in this book – including no-bake recipes! And each recipe has been thoroughly tried, tested and loved.

Let's face it, of all the things there are to make at home, baked treats, breads and cakes are by far the most fun and irresistible. When something sweet comes out of the oven, it's a party waiting to happen! Baking is so easy, and you can really put your own creative stamp on decorating. Home baking will not only save you a bundle on shop-bought food, it's also great for celebrating. A box of delicious, gooey cookies is always a very welcome gift, and a hand-made birthday cake will be remembered forever. Many recipes in this book are also perfect for slicing, wrapping and taking with you for a day on campus. Most baked goods can be frozen too, so you can keep things like sliced bread in the freezer for homemade toast, every day.

Don't worry if you're on a very tight budget. Basic items like flour and eggs cost so little, while for luxuries like chocolate simply buy what you can afford. Don't feel you have to splash out on premium brands. You also don't need loads of equipment in order to produce fantastic results and this book keeps what you need to a minimum.

Student life can be busy, but most baking is quick enough to fit easily into your schedule. Many of the muffin and cookie recipes can be taken from cupboard to plate in fewer than 40 minutes. So grab a wooden spoon and get baking! The toughest part will be keeping your friends' hands off your brownies.

# BAKING EQUIPMENT

You don't need loads of equipment to produce fantastic baked treats, but investing in a few simple pieces of kit will get you started. Many supermarkets sell cheap baking tins and utensils, or you might be able to borrow some from home. If you're a regular baker, it's worth getting reasonable-quality equipment that will last for longer, but this isn't essential. If buying new tins, go for non-stick, which makes life much easier.

**Large, medium and small mixing bowls**

**Microwaveable/heatproof bowl**
(ideally glass)

**Small saucepan**

**Muffin tray and/or fairy cake tray**

**900g loaf tin**

**Two 20cm round springform cake tins**

**20cm square cake tin**

**Two large baking sheets**

**1.5 litre-capacity ovenproof baking dish**
(Pyrex or ceramic are best)

**24cm pie dish or flan tin**

**Scales**
(electric are most accurate and not expensive)

**Wooden spoons**

**Set of measuring spoons**

**Silicone spatula**

**Whisk**
(go for the 'balloon' type)

**Pastry brush**
(ideally silicone)

**Large sieve**

**Measuring jug**

**Kitchen scissors**

**Cocktail sticks or metal skewer**

**Paper muffin or cake cases**

**Non-stick baking paper**
(ensure it is non-stick!)

**Sunflower oil**
(for greasing trays and tins, see page 13)

**Wire cooling rack**
(or use a clean shelf from the grill)

**Rolling pin**
(or use a clean, dry wine bottle)

**Oven gloves**
(or use a thick, folded tea towel)

**Baking beans**
(used to weigh down pastry while baking so it stays flat. Or use 500g dried lentils/beans)

**Hand-held electric whisk**
(not essential, but very helpful)

**Food colourings, sprinkles and other edible decorations**

# KEY BAKING INGREDIENTS

Baking is a chemical reaction between ingredients, so it's important to use the exact items listed and to measure them accurately. Most baked goods contain a combination of flour, fat and sugar, along with eggs and extra flavourings. Here's a quick guide to the building blocks of baking:

## FLOUR

There are many types of flour, including plain, self-raising, bread (or 'strong') flour, whole-meal, and specialist varieties such as spelt or seeded flour. Different recipes call for different flours for a reason, so always stick to the specified type. The major types can be found in all supermarkets and are very affordable – supermarket own-brand versions tend to be cheapest. It's best to sift flour before use (see page 12).

## RAISING AGENTS

Raising agents do exactly what they say on the tin: they get baked items to rise. They include baking powder, bicarbonate of soda and yeast. Each reacts differently with other ingredients, so it's important to use them exactly as directed. All three are widely available and not expensive. There are several varieties of yeast, but sachets of fast-action dried yeast are the easiest and used in all the bread recipes in this book. Yeast is actually a living thing and must be 'activated' for it to work. This is done by mixing it with warm water (or sometimes milk). It's important to make sure the water is warm enough to activate it, but not too hot or it will kill the yeast – around body temperature is right, so just test the water with your hand.

## FATS

Fats used in baking include butter, margarine and oil. Most recipes suggest butter, which tastes the nicest but is also the priciest, so if you're on a budget you might prefer to substitute cheaper baking margarine (although never do this for frostings or icings, or they really won't taste nice). If possible, save butter for biscuits, cookies, brownies and pastry, while margarine is perfectly good for cakes. Try to use unsalted butter, though salted is fine if it's all you have. If you are lactose intolerant, you can swap butter for a dairy-free spread.

Only use oil where specified as it behaves differently and isn't always interchangeable with butter or marg. Pure vegetable or sunflower oil are best in baking because they are almost flavourless and don't affect the final taste, so only use other oil types if specified. Oil and butter are also used for greasing tins (see page 13).

## SUGAR

Sugar is what makes cakes and bakes taste so delicious! It has lots of other jobs too, such as helping keep baked goods moist and light. There are so many types, including white, brown, caster, granulated, muscovado, demerara and icing sugar. White caster sugar is the most common, while brown sugars are often used to add a caramelly flavour or warmer colour to a cake. Icing sugar is used for frostings and icings. Different recipes call for different sugars for a reason, so always stick to the specified type. The major types can be found in all supermarkets and are very affordable – supermarket own-brand versions tend to be cheapest. Mix through before use to break up any clumps, and make sure to sift icing sugar (see page 12).

## EGGS

Egg sizes vary quite a bit, so do try to use the size recommended in each recipe. Buy the freshest eggs you can – pick those with the longest use-by date. The fresher they are, the better your baked items will turn out. Eggs are best kept in the fridge.

## VANILLA EXTRACT AND ESSENCE

These aren't the same thing! Vanilla extract is made from real vanilla beans and has the best flavour, but can be expensive. Vanilla essence (or 'flavouring') is a vanilla substitute. It's cheaper but the taste isn't as good, so let your budget dictate your choice – extract is always the better option if you can stretch to it. When using vanilla extract/essence in a recipe, always combine with the eggs before adding gradually to the main cake batter – this distributes it more evenly throughout the mixture.

## CHOCOLATE

The quality of chocolate varies enormously, from premium bars that are almost pure cocoa, to milk chocolate containing a high percentage of fat and sugar. When using chocolate for baking, you will definitely taste the difference if you go for a higher cocoa content – 70% cocoa solids is great – and use the best-quality chocolate you can afford for brownies and cakes in particular. If you prefer milk or white chocolate, by all means use them in cookies, but if melted into cakes that already contain fat and sugar, they can really spoil the outcome (remember that chocolate never tastes the same in baking as it does on its own).

Chocolate chips are convenient, but they are usually made with quite poor-quality chocolate and tend to be overpriced for the amount you get, so it's often better value to buy a bar of good-quality chocolate and chop it into chunks, then save leftovers for another time (or eat them!).

## ORANGES AND LEMONS

For orange or lemon zest, unwaxed fruits are best because waxed ones have normally been treated with pesticides and preservatives. Unwaxed fruits can be found in most large supermarkets, but if you can't get hold of them, scrub waxed citrus skins in warm soapy water to remove as much of the coating as possible. (It's fine to use the juice from waxed fruit, however.)

# TECHNIQUES AND TIPS

## BEFORE YOU BEGIN...

* Do a quick check to make sure you have all the right ingredients and equipment to hand. You don't want to have to rush out to the shops when you're halfway through a recipe.

* Baking is the more scientific side of cooking. To ensure your recipe works as it should, measure out your ingredients accurately and use the correct-sized tins.

* Read through the entire recipe from start to finish, so you know exactly what you need to do and when.

* Let all your ingredients come to room temperature before you start. This makes them easier to mix and will produce a better end result.

* Allow plenty of time and don't be tempted to rush. Some recipes take time for a reason.

## SIFTING

To pass a powdery ingredient through a sieve before use. It's recommended for flour to remove lumps, get air into the mixture and help give your baked goods a lighter texture. Sifting is also a way to combine fine ingredients evenly, such as sifting flour with baking powder, salt or cocoa powder. Icing sugar is also best sifted before use, to remove lumps. To sift, rest a large sieve over a mixing bowl and empty the flour or other ingredient into the sieve, being careful none falls down the sides straight into the bowl. Lift the sieve with one hand, keeping it low over the bowl, and tap it repeatedly with the other hand until all the grains have passed through. Alternatively you can use the back of a metal spoon to press the ingredient through the sieve.

## BEATING

To mix or stir vigorously using a wooden spoon, whisk or fork, in order to thoroughly combine ingredients. In most cake recipes, one of the first things you do is to beat together sugar and softened butter until combined, pale and fluffy. When a recipe specifies 'beaten' eggs, the goal is normally just to combine the whites and yolks, rather than to incorporate air (this is referred to as whisking instead – see below).

## FOLDING

To mix ingredients gently and gradually, using a large metal spoon or flat spatula to sweep through the mixture in a gentle figure-of-eight motion, until the ingredients are combined. The goal is keep as much air in the mixture as possible. Flour is usually folded into cake mixtures to keep them light.

## WHISKING

To beat vigorously with a whisk to trap air in a mixture and make it light. There are several levels of whisking. If the recipe simply says 'whisk', just give the ingredients a quick whisk to combine and make them light and bubbly. Cream or eggs are often whisked to 'soft peaks' or 'stiff peaks'. Soft peaks are when the mixture begins to thicken – if you lift the whisk out it should leave a soft, floppy peak. Stiff peaks are when the mixture becomes really thick and firm – lifting the whisk out should leave a firm, defined peak, and the mixture will stay in place when the bowl is turned upside down. (You do need to be confident it is this firm before turning the bowl over or you'll just end up with a mess!) Whisking is best done with the right tool – a 'balloon' whisk is ideal for baking (see photo on page 13) or an electric whisk is very helpful when whisking to 'peaks'.

## KNEADING

To work and stretch dough firmly using your hands, until it becomes smooth, soft and elastic. Place your dough on a lightly floured work surface. Lightly dust your hands in flour, then push the dough away from you with the ball of one hand, stretching it out across the surface, then pull the far end back towards you with your fingertips, rolling the dough back into a rough ball. Repeat this motion, kneading for the time specified in the recipe.

## GREASING AND LINING TINS

Preparing tins properly ensures your cakes and bakes won't stick, and your hard work isn't ruined. For greasing, the cheapest option is a flavourless oil (such as sunflower or vegetable). Drizzle a tiny amount into the tin and wipe it around with kitchen towel or a pastry brush in a thin, even coating over the entire inside surface. You can also use butter (spread with the butter wrapper, baking paper or kitchen towel). Make sure you grease all nooks and crannies.

For bread, grease your loaf tin or baking sheet with oil, as the high temperatures in these recipes can cause butter to burn. Once greased, sprinkle the tin or baking sheet evenly with a handful of flour and tip away any excess. This helps a crunchy crust develop.

For cakes, biscuits and traybakes, grease your tray or tin and then line it with non-stick baking paper (non-stick is important or it can be difficult to peel off once baked). Greasing the tin first keeps the paper in place so it doesn't flop into the mixture and leave bumps or undercooked areas. To cut baking paper to size, draw around your tin with a pencil, then cut out the shape and lay in the base. Then cut long, wide strips to go around or along the sides; the paper should stick up a couple of centimetres higher than the top of the tin. Crumpled paper causes uneven baking, so cut carefully, position neatly and smooth out any air bubbles.

## HOW FULL SHOULD YOUR TIN BE?

For big cakes, loaf cakes and traybakes, never fill your tin more than two-thirds full or the mixture will spill out while cooking and you'll end up with a misshapen bake and burnt batter all over your oven! For muffins and cupcakes, you can fill the paper cases three-quarters full, but don't be tempted to go any higher. Bread is different, because kneaded dough often rises to the top of the tin before it even reaches the oven, so just make sure to follow the instructions in the recipe. But for breads with a really runny batter that is poured into a tin, follow the two-thirds rule as above.

# IS IT COOKED?

Every oven is different, so always test cakes and bakes using the methods below after the minimum time stated in the recipe. Don't be tempted to open the oven door any earlier – letting cold air in too soon causes cakes to sink.

## BIG CAKES, LOAF CAKES AND TRAYBAKES
(except brownies/blondies)

To see if these are cooked, you can use the 'cocktail stick test'. Insert a cocktail stick or skewer into the centre, right down to the tin. Pull it out and have a look. If there's any liquid mixture stuck to it, your cake isn't ready and needs more time in the oven. Give shallow cakes another 3 minutes before testing again, and give deeper cakes another 5 minutes. They might need still more time than this, but continue to test at these intervals, returning to the oven until done. Once the cocktail stick comes out clean, or with just tiny crumbs attached, the cake is ready. If unsure, test with a clean cocktail stick in another part of the cake. If still in doubt, return the cake to the oven as above – it's better to end up with a cake that's a tiny bit dry than raw in the middle. Once cooked, leave to cool in the tin for at least 20 minutes as cakes can be fragile. Then remove from the tin, peel off the baking paper and place on a wire rack to cool fully. If adding icing, the cake must be completely cool beforehand, or the icing will melt and run everywhere.

## BROWNIES AND BLONDIES

These have a moist gooey centre, so the cocktail stick test doesn't work. They rarely need more than the minimum cooking time, but just check there's no wobble by gently shaking the tray. When ready, a firm, papery-looking crust will have formed on top. Let them cool in the tin for at least 30 minutes (but ideally 1 hour) to firm up. Then remove from the tin whole, peel off the baking paper and cool on a wire rack. Wait until completely cool before slicing.

## MUFFINS, CUPCAKES AND FAIRY CAKES

The cocktail stick test isn't necessary here, as there's less risk of a raw centre. Instead, check they're lightly browned, well risen and spring back up when gently pressed. If not, return to the oven for 3–5 minutes until they are. Once cooked, leave to cool in the tray for at least 20 minutes as they can be easily damaged, then transfer to a wire rack to cool fully. If adding icing, the cakes must be completely cool beforehand, or the icing will melt and run everywhere.

## COOKIES AND BISCUITS

When ready, cookies should be lightly browned and firm around the edges – but with a bit of give in the centre when gently pressed. They will firm up as they cool, so remove from the oven while still slightly soft. Biscuits are supposed to be crisper than cookies, so should feel firm and look lightly browned. Once done, allow biscuits and cookies to firm up on the tray for 10 minutes, then transfer to a wire rack to cool further. They can be eaten whilst still warm, but give them at least 20 minutes more so they don't burn your tongue, especially if there is molten chocolate in them!

### BREADS AND ROLLS

To test if breads are cooked enough, tap them on the base (except cornbread, for which you can use the cocktail stick test, see opposite). If cooked in a tin, you'll need to carefully remove first using oven gloves. Hold the hot bread with a cloth and give the bottom a light knock. It should sound hollow inside. If not, return to the tin or tray and place back in the oven for 5 minutes before testing again. You might need to repeat this test a couple of times. Once your bread is done, remove from the tin or baking tray straight away and place on a wire rack to prevent the crust becoming soggy. Leave for at least 30 minutes before slicing.

### BAKED DESSERTS

Desserts containing fruit, such as cobblers, crumbles, strudels and pies, are ready when the fruit is bubbling underneath the topping, and the topping, whether meringue, crumble or pastry, is lightly browned and firm to the touch. Serve straight away.

## LOVE YOUR OVEN

Every oven is different, so get to know yours. Some run hotter and others run cooler than the temperature they're set to. This doesn't have to be a problem, you just need to get used to it. Follow this advice to get the best from your oven:

* Most modern ovens are electric (in degrees centigrade – generally 50–240°C). If yours is electric, look inside to see if it has a fan at the back (these days most do). If so, use the temperatures given throughout this book. If your electric oven doesn't have a fan, add 20°C to the stated cooking temperatures. And just in case you have a gas oven, the recipes also give temperatures in gas marks.

* Always preheat the oven well before you need to put your food in. Most have a thermostat light that comes on when you turn on the oven, and goes out when it reaches the correct temperature. Watch this the first time you use the oven and note how long it takes. If particularly slow, you may need to preheat your oven sooner.

* Keep a close eye on the cooking time. Where a recipe stipulates a range (e.g. 20–30 minutes), always check and test after the minimum (in this case 20 minutes) and, if required, return the food to the oven for some or all of the remaining time. This will ensure your cakes don't burn. It's worth bearing in mind that some ovens are just way out, and recipes can take much, much longer. It is useful to scribble a note by the recipe of the actual time it ended up taking so you have this information handy for next time.

# SMALL BAKES

# VANILLA CUPCAKES

**Makes: 12 cupcakes or 18 fairy cakes**

These light, fluffy cupcakes are perfect topped with Vanilla Buttercream (page 38). A plate of iced cupcakes makes a great alternative to a birthday cake. Decorate with sprinkles to make them extra special.

115g butter, softened
225g caster sugar
2 large eggs
1 tsp vanilla extract
175g self-raising flour
125ml milk
Vanilla Buttercream, if using (page 38)

Muffin or fairy cake tray(s)
Paper cases

For techniques in **bold** see pages 12–13.

* Preheat the oven to 170°C Fan/Gas Mark 5. Line your muffin or fairy cake tray with the appropriately sized paper cases.

* In a large mixing bowl, **beat** together the butter and sugar until pale and fluffy.

* **Whisk** the eggs and vanilla extract together in a small bowl, then add this to the butter and sugar mixture a little at a time. Beat well after each addition.

* **Sift** the flour into the bowl and gently **fold** in.

* Pour in the milk and mix gently to form a smooth batter.

* Spoon the mixture into the cake cases. If you plan to frost your cupcakes, make sure that you only fill the cake cases about halfway up, otherwise the cakes will be too tall to frost easily.

* Bake in the oven for 20–25 minutes for cupcakes or 15–20 minutes for fairy cakes until risen and a nice light brown on top. The sponge should spring back when pressed lightly with your finger.

* Allow the cakes to cool fully on a wire rack before frosting.

* Store in an airtight container and eat within 3–5 days. If iced, store in the fridge. Once cool, can be frozen un-iced in sealed freezer bags for up to 3 months.

# DOUBLE CHOCOLATE CHIP MUFFINS

**Makes: 12 large muffins or 24 fairy cake-sized muffins**

If you love chocolate, these muffins are perfect for you. They taste rich and indulgent, but are light in texture.

250g plain flour
1 tsp baking powder
Pinch of salt
50g cocoa powder
225g caster sugar
100g chocolate chips
1 large egg, beaten
265ml full-fat milk
100ml sunflower oil

Muffin or fairy cake tray(s)
Paper cases

For techniques in **bold** see pages 12–13.

* Preheat the oven to 170°C Fan/Gas Mark 5. Line your muffin or fairy cake tray with the appropriately sized paper cases.

* **Sift** the flour, baking powder, salt and cocoa powder into a mixing bowl. Add the sugar and stir well.

* Add the chocolate chips, beaten egg, milk and oil and stir gently to just combine the ingredients. The mixture will be lumpy, but resist the temptation to overmix as this can cause the muffins to turn out dense and heavy.

* Bake for 18–22 minutes for muffins and 15–18 minutes for fairy cakes until they are well risen and the sponge springs back when pressed lightly with your finger.

* Allow to cool on a wire rack, although they are also nice eaten while still warm.

* Store in an airtight container and eat within 2–3 days. Once cool, can be frozen in sealed freezer bags for up to 3 months.

# RED VELVET CUPCAKES

**Makes: 12 cupcakes or 16 fairy cakes**

A classic American treat, these cupcakes look stunning with their red, chocolatey sponge and gorgeous cream cheese frosting. Simply sprinkle some cake crumbs on top for an easy decoration.

125ml milk

1 tsp lemon juice

110g butter, softened

175g caster sugar

1 tsp vanilla extract

2 large eggs, beaten

175g plain flour

20g cocoa powder

1 tsp bicarbonate of soda

Pinch of salt

½ tsp red gel food colouring

½ quantity of Cream Cheese Frosting, if using (page 38)

Muffin or fairy cake tray(s)
Paper cases

For techniques in **bold** see pages 12–13.

* Preheat the oven to 170°C Fan/Gas Mark 5. Line your muffin or fairy cake tray with the appropriately sized paper cases.

* Place the milk in a measuring jug and add the lemon juice. Stir and set aside.

* In a large mixing bowl, **beat** together the butter and sugar until pale and fluffy.

* **Whisk** the vanilla extract into the beaten eggs, then add to the butter and sugar mixture a little at a time, stirring well after each addition.

* **Sift** in the flour, cocoa powder, bicarbonate of soda and salt and gently **fold** into the mixture.

* Pour in the milk and lemon juice and stir in, followed by the food colouring.

* Spoon the batter evenly into the cake cases and bake for 25–30 minutes for cupcakes and 20–25 minutes for fairy cakes until risen and lightly browned. The sponge should spring back when pressed lightly with your finger.

* Allow the cakes to cool fully on a wire rack before adding the frosting, if using.

* Slice off a tiny amount of each domed top and set aside. Top the cakes with the frosting, then crumble up the reserved sponge and scatter over the cakes to decorate.

* Store in an airtight container and eat within 3–5 days. If iced, store in the fridge. Once cool, can be frozen un-iced in sealed freezer bags for up to 3 months.

# CHERRY AND COCONUT MUFFINS

**Makes: 8 muffins or 12 fairy cake-sized muffins**

These are light, buttery muffins, packed with coconut and colourful red cherries. This is a great recipe to try if you are new to baking, as they're really simple to make.

110g butter, softened
110g caster sugar
2 large eggs
110g self-raising flour
½ tsp baking powder
125g glacé cherries
100g desiccated coconut

Muffin or fairy cake tray(s)
Paper cases

For techniques in **bold** see pages 12–13.

* Preheat the oven to 170°C Fan/Gas Mark 5. Line your muffin or fairy cake tray with the appropriately sized paper cases.

* In a large mixing bowl, **beat** together the butter and sugar until pale and fluffy.

* **Whisk** the eggs in a cup or small bowl, then add to the butter and sugar mixture a little at a time. Beat well after each addition.

* **Sift** in the flour and baking powder and gently **fold** in until combined.

* Finally, add the cherries and coconut and stir in.

* Spoon the mixture into the prepared cake cases and bake for 20–25 minutes for muffins and 15–20 minutes for fairy cakes, until they are risen and golden brown, and the sponge springs back when pressed lightly with a finger.

* Allow to cool on a wire rack.

* Store in an airtight container and eat within 3–5 days. Once cool, can be frozen in sealed freezer bags for up to 3 months.

# PUMPKIN AND ORANGE MUFFINS

**Makes: 12 muffins or 16 fairy cake-sized muffins**

These muffins are sweet, fruity and light in texture. The pumpkin softens as it cooks and almost melts into the sponge. Perfect for Halloween!

3 large eggs
200g caster sugar
125ml vegetable oil
200g self-raising flour
1 tsp baking powder
½ tsp bicarbonate of soda
Finely grated zest
of 2 large oranges
2 tbsp orange juice
200g peeled and finely
grated pumpkin

Muffin or fairy cake tray(s)
Paper cases

For techniques in **bold**
see pages 12–13.

**Tip:** If you can't get hold of pumpkin, butternut squash works very well instead.

* Preheat the oven to 180°C Fan/Gas Mark 6. Line your muffin or fairy cake tray with the appropriately sized paper cases.

* Place the eggs, sugar and oil into a large mixing bowl and **whisk** vigorously for around 5 minutes until pale and bubbly on the surface.

* **Sift** in the flour, baking powder and bicarbonate of soda, add the orange zest and juice, and grated pumpkin, and mix lightly until combined. Be careful not to overmix as this can cause the muffins to turn out dense and heavy.

* Pour the mixture into the prepared cake cases and bake for 25–30 minutes for muffins or 20–22 minutes for fairy cakes.

* Allow to cool on a wire rack and then eat immediately.

* Store in an airtight container and eat within 3–5 days. Once cool, can be frozen in sealed freezer bags for up to 3 months.

# MOCHA SWIRL MUFFINS

**Makes: 12 muffins or 16 fairy cake-sized muffins**

Chocolate and coffee is such a delicious combination. These swirled muffins taste gorgeous and look great too.

250g butter, softened

250g caster sugar

4 medium eggs, beaten

250g self-raising flour

1 heaped tbsp cocoa powder

1 tbsp espresso powder

Muffin or fairy cake tray(s)

Paper cases

For techniques in **bold** see pages 12–13.

**Tip:** Don't be tempted to use ground coffee. Espresso powder, which is instant espresso, is what you want here.

* Preheat the oven to 170°C Fan/Gas Mark 5. Line your muffin or fairy cake tray with the appropriately sized paper cases.

* In a large mixing bowl, **beat** together the butter and sugar until pale and fluffy.

* Add the beaten eggs to the butter and sugar mixture a little at a time. Beat well after every addition.

* When all the egg has been added, **sift** in the flour and gently **fold** into the mixture.

* Now, take a second mixing bowl and transfer half the mixture into it, ensuring the batter is divided evenly between the two.

* Sift the cocoa powder into one of the bowls. Gently fold in until it is well mixed through. Add the espresso powder to the other bowl of mixture and, again, mix in gently and evenly.

* Tip the espresso-flavoured mixture very gently into the cocoa-flavoured mixture and fold the two together just a couple of times before spooning the mixture generously into the cake cases. Use a cocktail stick to lightly swirl the mixtures together in each case.

* Bake for 20–25 minutes for muffins and 16–18 minutes for fairy cakes, until they are risen and the sponge springs back when pressed lightly with your finger. Allow to cool fully on a wire rack.

* Store in an airtight container and eat within 3–5 days. Once cool, can be frozen in sealed freezer bags for up to 3 months.

# CRANBERRY AND ORANGE MUFFINS

**Makes: 12 muffins or 16 fairy cake-sized muffins**

These zesty, fruity muffins are a tasty treat at any time of the day and can be made using mostly store-cupboard ingredients. Dried cranberries are widely available in supermarkets and health food shops, or you could even use fresh or frozen cranberries instead, if you can get hold of them.

4 large eggs

110ml sunflower oil

200g caster sugar

Grated zest and juice of 3 oranges

335g self-raising flour

1 tbsp baking powder

180g dried cranberries

8 tbsp demerara sugar (optional)

Muffin or fairy cake tray(s)

Paper cases

For techniques in **bold** see pages 12–13.

* Preheat the oven to 180°C Fan/Gas Mark 6. Line your muffin or fairy cake tray with the appropriately sized paper cases.

* Place the eggs, oil, sugar, orange zest and juice in a bowl and **whisk** well.

* **Sift** in the flour and baking powder and **fold** in gently. Be careful not to overmix as this can cause the muffins to turn out dense and heavy. The batter will be very wet – that's fine.

* Add the dried cranberries and mix in gently.

* Divide the mixture evenly among the cake cases and sprinkle each muffin with demerara sugar, if using.

* Bake for 22–28 minutes for muffins and 16–20 minutes for fairy cakes until they are well risen and golden brown, and the sponge springs back when pressed lightly with your finger.

* Allow the cakes to cool on a wire rack before eating.

* Store in an airtight container and eat within 3–5 days. Once cool, can be frozen in sealed freezer bags for up to 3 months.

# CARROT, APPLE AND SULTANA MUFFINS

**Makes: 12 muffins or 18 fairy cake-sized muffins**

Packed full of healthy ingredients, these muffins are really tasty and filling. The grated carrot and apple makes them moist, sweet and nutritious, ideal for any time of day.

300g self-raising flour

1 tsp baking powder

1 tbsp ground cinnamon

Pinch of salt

275g caster sugar

4 medium eggs

150ml sunflower oil

1 tbsp vanilla extract

200g peeled and grated carrot

225g peeled and grated apple

100g sultanas

**Muffin or fairy cake tray(s)**

**Paper cases**

For techniques in **bold** see pages 12–13.

* Preheat the oven to 170°C Fan/Gas Mark 5. Line your muffin or fairy cake tray with the appropriately sized paper cases.

* **Sift** the flour, baking powder, cinnamon and salt into a large mixing bowl, add the sugar, and stir to combine.

* Place the eggs, oil and vanilla extract into a jug and **whisk** well.

* Stir the grated carrot, apple and sultanas into the wet mixture and pour the lot into the dry mixture in the mixing bowl, then stir gently to combine. Be careful not to overmix as this can cause the muffins to turn out dense and heavy.

* Spoon the mixture into the cake cases and bake for 20–25 minutes for muffins or 18–20 minutes for fairy cakes, until risen and golden brown, and the sponge springs back when pressed lightly with your finger.

* Allow to cool on a wire rack.

* Store in an airtight container and eat within 3–5 days. Once cool, can be frozen in sealed freezer bags for up to 3 months.

**Tip:** These muffins freeze very well. They can be made in advance, frozen, and then taken out of the freezer the night before needed, to defrost in time for breakfast.

# SWEET SCONES

**Makes: 8–12, depending on cutter size**

Homemade scones are much cheaper and a lot nicer than bought ones. They are also quick and simple to make, and great to serve to a group of friends with a cup of tea.

**Vegetable oil or butter, for greasing**

**220g self-raising flour, plus extra for the work surface**

**Pinch of salt**

**35g caster sugar**

**55g butter, chilled and cubed**

**150ml milk, plus extra for brushing**

**Large baking sheet**
**Rolling pin (or wine bottle)**
**Round cookie cutter (or glass)**

For techniques in **bold** see pages 12–13.

* Preheat the oven to 220°C Fan/Gas Mark 9. Grease a large baking sheet well.

* **Sift** the flour and salt into a large mixing bowl, add the sugar and stir in until evenly mixed.

* Add the butter to the bowl and rub it into the other ingredients with your fingertips until the mixture looks like breadcrumbs.

* Pour in the milk, then gently stir in. The mixture will start to come together to form a stiff but soft dough.

* Now use your hands to bring the dough together into a ball, taking care to handle the dough gently.

* Make sure the work surface is clean and then sprinkle well with flour. Tip the dough out onto the floured surface and **knead** very gently for a minute.

* Using a rolling pin or clean wine bottle, roll out the dough to 2.5cm thick and cut out scones using a round cutter, or a clean drinking glass.

* Place the scones onto the prepared baking sheet and brush lightly with milk. If you do not have a brush, just dab it on with your fingers.

* Bake the scones for 12–15 minutes until they are lightly golden. Enjoy while still warm.

* Store in an airtight container and eat within 1–2 days. Once cool, can be frozen in sealed freezer bags for up to 3 months.

# CHILLI CHOCOLATE CUPCAKES

**Makes: 12 cupcakes or 18 fairy cakes**

The perfect cakes for anyone who likes a bit of spice, these are a light chocolate sponge with a cheeky chilli kick! Delicious iced with Chocolate Ganache frosting (page 40).

115g butter, softened

225g caster sugar

2 large eggs

1 tsp vanilla extract

140g self-raising flour

35g cocoa powder

1 tsp hot chilli powder, plus a little extra for sprinkling

125ml milk

Chocolate Ganache frosting, if using (page 40)

**Muffin or fairy cake tray(s)**

**Paper cases**

For techniques in **bold** see pages 12–13.

* Preheat the oven to 160°C Fan/Gas Mark 4. Line your muffin or fairy cake tray with the appropriately sized paper cases.

* In a large mixing bowl, **beat** together the butter and sugar until pale and fluffy.

* **Whisk** the eggs and vanilla extract together in a small bowl, then add them to the butter and sugar mixture a little at a time. Beat well after each addition.

* **Sift** the flour, cocoa powder and chilli powder into the bowl and gently **fold** in.

* Pour in the milk and mix gently to form a smooth batter.

* Spoon the mixture into the cake cases. If you plan to frost your cupcakes, make sure you only fill your cake cases about halfway up, otherwise the cakes will be too tall to frost easily.

* Bake in the oven for 20–25 minutes for cupcakes and 15–20 minutes for fairy cakes, until they are well risen and the sponge springs back when pressed lightly with your finger.

* Allow the cakes to cool fully on a wire rack before covering with the Chocolate Ganache frosting (page 40). Sprinkle with chilli powder for an extra kick.

* Store in an airtight container and eat within 3–5 days. If iced, store in the fridge. Once cool, can be frozen un-iced in sealed freezer bags for up to 3 months.

# BLACK BOTTOM CUPCAKES

**Makes: 12 cupcakes or 16 fairy cakes**

Why choose between chocolate and vanilla when you can have both? These two-tone cupcakes look great. And with different flavours top and bottom, they definitely taste twice as nice!

115g butter, softened

225g caster sugar

2 large eggs

175g self-raising flour

125ml milk

50g chocolate chips

1 tsp vanilla extract

20g cocoa powder, plus extra for dusting

Cream Cheese Frosting, if using (page 38)

Muffin or fairy cake tray(s)

Paper cases

For techniques in **bold** see pages 12–13.

* Preheat the oven to 170°C Fan/Gas Mark 5. Line your muffin or fairy cake tray with the appropriately sized paper cases.

* In a large mixing bowl, **beat** together the butter and sugar until pale and fluffy.

* **Whisk** the eggs in a small bowl, then add to the butter and sugar mixture a little at a time. Beat well after each addition.

* **Sift** the flour into the bowl and gently **fold** in.

* Pour in the milk and mix gently to form a smooth batter, then add the chocolate chips and stir in.

* Now transfer a third of the mixture into another bowl. Pour the vanilla extract into this smaller portion of mixture and stir in well. Sift the cocoa powder into the larger portion of mixture and gently fold in until evenly combined.

* Now, spoon the two mixtures into the cake cases, starting with the chocolate mixture and dividing it evenly among the cases. Then add a smaller spoonful of the vanilla mixture on top, again dividing this evenly among the cake cases.

* Bake in the oven for 20–25 minutes for cupcakes and 15–20 minutes for fairy cakes, until the cakes are risen and a nice light brown on top. The sponge should spring back when pressed lightly with your finger.

* Allow them to cool fully on a wire rack before covering with Cream Cheese Frosting (page 38) and dusting with cocoa powder.

* Store in an airtight container and eat within 3–5 days. If iced, store in the fridge. Once cool, can be frozen un-iced in sealed freezer bags for up to 3 months.

# MARGARITA CUPCAKES

Makes: 12 cupcakes or 18 fairy cakes

Inspired by the famous tequila cocktail, these zesty, boozy cupcakes really capture the flavour of the drink and are great fun to make for parties and celebrations. You can use the rest of the bottle for cocktails (salt and lime wedges optional)!

### For the cakes

115g butter, softened

225g caster sugar

Finely grated zest of 2 limes, plus extra to decorate

2 large eggs

175g self-raising flour

2 tsp lime juice

2 tsp tequila

2 tsp Cointreau or orange juice

### For the frosting

115g unsalted butter, softened

500g icing sugar, sifted

¼ tsp lime juice

1 tsp tequila

1 tsp Cointreau or orange juice

Muffin or fairy cake tray(s)

Paper cases

For techniques in **bold** see pages 12–13.

* Preheat the oven to 170°C Fan/Gas Mark 5. Line your muffin or fairy cake tray with the appropriately sized paper cases.

* In a large mixing bowl, **beat** together the butter, sugar and lime zest until pale and fluffy. This may take a little while as there is a lot of sugar in this recipe.

* **Whisk** the eggs in a small bowl, then add to the butter and sugar mixture a little at a time. Beat well after each addition.

* **Sift** the flour into the bowl and gently **fold** in, followed by the lime juice, tequila and Cointreau or orange juice, and mix gently to form a smooth batter.

* Spoon the mixture into the cake cases. If you plan to frost your cupcakes, make sure that you only fill the cake cases about halfway up, otherwise the cakes will be too tall to frost easily.

* Bake in the oven for 20–25 minutes for cupcakes and 15–20 minutes for fairy cakes until the cakes are risen and a nice light brown on top. The sponge should spring back when pressed lightly with your finger.

* Allow the cakes to cool fully on a wire rack.

* To make the frosting, place the butter in a large mixing bowl and mix with roughly a third of the icing sugar until thoroughly combined and no longer dry. Gradually add another third of the sugar and mix until well combined. Finally, add the remaining sugar and mix in, then beat in the lime juice, tequila and Cointreau or orange juice. Mix well until smooth and creamy.

* Ice the cakes and sprinkle with a little grated lime zest.

* Store in an airtight container and eat within 3–5 days. If iced, store in the fridge. Once cool, can be frozen un-iced in sealed freezer bags for up to 3 months.

# CHERRY CHOCOLATE CUPCAKES

**Makes: 12 cupcakes or 18 fairy cakes**

Decadent, yet simple to make, these cupcakes are perfect for anyone with a sweet tooth. They are great iced with Chocolate Ganache frosting (page 40).

115g butter, softened

225g caster sugar

2 large eggs

1 tsp vanilla extract

140g self-raising flour

35g cocoa powder

125ml milk

75g glacé cherries, halved

Chocolate Ganache frosting, if using (page 40)

Muffin or fairy cake tray(s)

Paper cases

For techniques in **bold** see pages 12–13.

**Tip:** You can use drained, pitted cherries from a jar as an alternative to glacé ones.

* Preheat the oven to 170°C Fan/Gas Mark 5. Line your muffin or fairy cake tray with the appropriately sized paper cases.

* In a large mixing bowl, **beat** together the butter and sugar until pale and fluffy.

* **Whisk** the eggs and vanilla extract together in a small bowl, then add them to the butter and sugar mixture a little at a time. Beat well after each addition.

* **Sift** the flour and cocoa powder into the bowl and gently **fold** in.

* Pour in the milk, add the cherries and mix gently to form a smooth batter.

* Spoon the mixture into the cake cases. If you plan to frost your cupcakes, make sure you only fill your cake cases about halfway up, otherwise the cakes will be too tall to frost easily.

* Bake in the oven for 20–25 minutes for cupcakes and 15–20 minutes for fairy cakes, until they are well risen and the sponge springs back when pressed lightly with your finger.

* Allow to cool fully on a wire rack before covering with the Chocolate Ganache frosting (page 40).

* Store in an airtight container and eat within 3–5 days. Once cool, can be frozen in sealed freezer bags for up to 3 months.

# VANILLA BUTTERCREAM

**Makes: enough to frost 12 cupcakes, 18 fairy cakes or 2 large round cakes**

Only use real butter for this, as margarine and other spreads won't taste very nice. Ensure the butter is really soft before you begin - it makes the buttercream much easier to mix. You can add a few drops of food colouring at the end if you want coloured buttercream.

115g unsalted butter, softened
500g icing sugar, sifted
55ml milk
1 tsp vanilla extract
A few drops of food colouring (optional)

For techniques in **bold** see pages 12–13.

* In a large mixing bowl, mix the butter with roughly a third of the icing sugar until thoroughly combined and no longer dry.

* Gradually add another third of the sugar and mix until well combined.

* Finally, add the remaining icing sugar and mix in, then **beat** in the milk and vanilla extract.

* Mix well until smooth and creamy and the ingredients are well combined. Mix in some food colouring if you like.

* Frost your cakes immediately.

# CREAM CHEESE FROSTING

**Makes: enough to frost 12 cupcakes, 18 fairy cakes or 1 large round cake**

This classic cake topping is sweet and creamy and can be used on many cakes in this book, large or small. It's especially good on Carrot Cake (page 58) or Wholemeal Banana Bread (page 87) as it really complements the flavour of the sponge.

50g unsalted butter, softened
125g full-fat cream cheese
300g icing sugar

For techniques in **bold** see pages 12–13.

* Place the butter and cream cheese into a bowl and **beat** together.

* **Sift** the icing sugar into a separate bowl and add to the butter and cream cheese mixture a few spoonfuls at a time. Beat the sugar in well.

* When all the sugar has been incorporated, continue to beat the mixture for a further 2 minutes to ensure it is smooth before frosting your cakes.

# CHOCOLATE FUDGE ICING

**Makes: enough to ice 12 cupcakes, 16 fairy cakes or
the Chocolate Birthday Cake (page 66)**

Thick, chocolatey and highly addictive, this is the perfect icing
for both large and small cakes. Slathered on top of the Chocolate
Birthday Cake (page 66), it will go a long way towards making a
birthday very happy indeed!

**350g dark chocolate chunks**

**270g icing sugar, sifted**

**185g butter, softened**

**2 tbsp milk**

For techniques in **bold**
see pages 12–13.

* Begin by melting the chocolate. You can do this in a non-
  metallic bowl in the microwave (make sure you check it every
  20 seconds so that it doesn't burn) or in a heatproof bowl set
  over a small saucepan of simmering water (stir frequently
  and check the water isn't actually in contact with the bottom
  of the bowl).

* Once the chocolate is melted, remove from the heat and leave
  to cool for 10 minutes, stirring occasionally.

* Meanwhile, place the **sifted** icing sugar and butter together
  in a large mixing bowl. **Beat** together gently until combined.

* Add the milk and beat in well, then pour in the cooled melted
  chocolate and mix together.

* Now, place the icing into a bowl, cover and refrigerate for a
  minimum of an hour before using.

* When you are ready to ice your cake or cakes, remove the
  frosting from the fridge, leave it for 10 minutes and then beat
  vigorously until really smooth. An electric mixer helps here.
  Frost your cakes immediately.

# CHOCOLATE GANACHE

**Makes: enough to frost 12 cupcakes or 18 fairy cakes**

This indulgent topping is perfect for icing the Chilli Chocolate Cupcakes (page 30) or Cherry Chocolate Cupcakes (page 37).

**110g dark chocolate, broken up into pieces**

**100ml double cream**

For techniques in **bold** see pages 12–13.

* Melt the chocolate in a heatproof bowl set over a pan of barely simmering water, making sure the water does not touch the bottom of the bowl. Stir until melted.

* Remove the bowl from the heat and allow to cool slightly.

* Make sure the cakes you are icing are cool. **Whisk** the cream into the chocolate and then use the ganache to ice the cakes immediately. Place in the fridge to set.


# SIMPLE WATER ICING

**Makes: enough to ice 10 cupcakes, 16 fairy cakes or 1 loaf cake**

This is a foolproof and quick-to-make icing, which can be used on all manner of cakes and sets quickly to a shiny glaze.

**150g icing sugar**

**1 tbsp water**

**A few drops of food colouring (optional)**

For techniques in **bold** see pages 12–13.

* **Sift** the icing sugar into a large bowl.

* Gently and gradually pour in the water and mix well until smooth.

* Add a few drops of food colouring if you want coloured icing, and mix in. Pour or spread the icing over your cake immediately and allow to set.

**LEMON WATER ICING**
Replace the water with 1 tablespoon of freshly squeezed lemon juice. You can add the grated zest of an unwaxed lemon too, to intensify the flavour.

**ORANGE WATER ICING**
Replace the water with 1 tablespoon of freshly squeezed orange juice and add the grated zest of one orange. (You can get away with using good-quality unsweetened orange juice from a carton and omitting the zest if you don't have any oranges to hand.)

# BIG CAKES

# VICTORIA SPONGE

**Serves: 6–8**

This classic recipe is a great place to start if you are new to baking. A Victoria sponge is traditionally filled with jam, but you can also add buttercream, whipped cream or fresh fruit such as summer berries, or you can swap the jam for lemon curd.

Vegetable oil or butter,
for greasing
250g caster sugar
250g butter, softened
5 medium eggs
2 tsp vanilla extract
250g self-raising flour
2 tsp baking powder
Jam of your choice, to fill
150ml double cream, to fill
Icing sugar, for dusting

Two 20cm round cake tins
Non-stick baking paper

For techniques in **bold**
see pages 12–13.

* Preheat the oven to 170°C Fan/Gas Mark 5. Grease two 20cm round cake tins and line with non-stick baking paper. Set aside.

* In a mixing bowl, **beat** together the sugar and butter until pale and fluffy.

* In a separate bowl, **whisk** the eggs with the vanilla extract, then pour a little at a time into the sugar and butter. Beat well after every addition until all the egg mixture is combined.

* **Sift** in the flour and baking powder and **fold** in lightly.

* Pour the mixture into the tins and bake for 30–35 minutes until the cakes are risen and golden brown. Test to check if the cakes are cooked by inserting a skewer or cocktail stick into the centre of each. If it comes out clean, they are done. If not, return the cakes to the oven for another 3 minutes and then test again.

* Leave the cakes to cool for 30 minutes in the tin before removing and leaving to cool fully on a wire rack.

* Once the cakes are cooled fully, spread the top of one cake with the jam of your choice. Then whisk the double cream until it forms soft peaks, and spread on top of the jam. Place the other cake on top, and dust with icing sugar.

* Store in an airtight container and eat within 3–5 days. If filled with buttercream, lemon curd or cream, store in the fridge. Once cool, can be frozen in sealed freezer bags for up to 3 months.

# APPLE, SULTANA AND WALNUT CAKE

Serves: 8

With wholemeal flour, nuts and fruit, you can kid yourself that this is actually quite healthy! It keeps really well in an airtight container, so it's good for a teatime treat for a few days.

Vegetable oil or butter, for greasing

110g plain flour

100g wholemeal flour

½ tsp bicarbonate of soda

125g butter, chilled and cubed

225g caster sugar

2 large eggs, beaten

1 tsp vanilla extract

50g chopped walnuts

90g sultanas

3 medium eating apples, peeled, cored and cut into 1cm dice

20cm round cake tin

Non-stick baking paper

For techniques in **bold** see pages 12–13.

* Preheat the oven to 170°C Fan/Gas Mark 5. Grease a 20cm round cake tin and line with non-stick baking paper. Set aside.

* **Sift** both types of flour and the bicarbonate of soda together into a large mixing bowl.

* Add the butter to the flour mixture and rub together using your fingertips, until the mixture resembles fine breadcrumbs.

* Stir in the sugar, eggs and vanilla extract and mix gently to combine.

* Add the walnuts, sultanas and apple cubes next, and stir again gently to mix them through evenly.

* Pour the mixture into the prepared tin and bake for 1 hour until the cake is risen and golden brown. Test to check if the cake is cooked by inserting a skewer or cocktail stick into the centre. If it comes out clean, the cake is done. If not, return it to the oven for a further 5 minutes and then test again.

* Cool in the tin for 20 minutes before turning the cake out of the tin and allowing to cool fully on a wire rack.

* Store in an airtight container and eat within 3–5 days. Once cool, can be frozen in sealed freezer bags for up to 3 months.

# SUNKEN APRICOT CAKE

**Serves: 8**

This light, fruity and elegant cake is so-called because, when baked, it looks as though all the apricots have sunk to the bottom. In reality, they are arranged in the base of the tin at the start and the sponge mixture is simply spooned on top of them. It's a super-easy method that is ideal for new bakers.

Vegetable oil or butter, for greasing

1 tin apricot halves in fruit juice (drained weight 240g)

135g butter, softened

135g caster sugar

1 tsp vanilla extract

2 large eggs, beaten

135g self-raising flour

1 tsp baking powder

20cm round cake tin

Non-stick baking paper

For techniques in **bold** see pages 12–13.

* Preheat the oven to 180°C Fan/Gas Mark 6. Grease a 20cm cake tin and line with non-stick baking paper. Set aside.

* Drain the apricot halves and lay them cut-side down in the bottom of the cake tin.

* In a large mixing bowl, **beat** together the butter and sugar until pale and fluffy.

* **Whisk** the vanilla extract into the egg mixture. Add this to the butter and sugar mixture a little at a time, beating well after each addition.

* When all the egg has been added, **sift** in the flour and baking powder and gently **fold** in.

* Carefully spoon the mixture over the top of the apricots in the tin. Use the back of a spoon or a spatula to ensure the cake batter is spread smoothly and is level.

* Bake for 25–30 minutes until risen and browned. Test to see if the cake is cooked by inserting a skewer or cocktail stick into the centre. If it comes out clean, the cake is cooked. If not, return it to the oven for a further 3 minutes and then test again.

* Once the cake is cooked, cool in the tin for 30 minutes before carefully removing from the tin and allowing the cake to cool fully on a wire rack.

* Store in an airtight container and eat within 3–5 days. Once cool, can be frozen in sealed freezer bags for up to 3 months.

# DORSET APPLE CAKE

**Serves: 8–10**

This is a very light traditional English teatime cake. The apple chunks are delicious with the lemon zest and sultanas. Make this using sweet eating apples, such as Cox, Jazz or Braeburn.

Vegetable oil or butter,
for greasing

300g apples
(approx. 3 small apples)

150g butter, softened

150g caster sugar, plus
1 tbsp extra for sprinkling

2 large eggs, beaten

300g self-raising flour

Grated zest of 1 lemon

75g sultanas

20cm round cake tin

Non-stick baking paper

For techniques in **bold**
see pages 12–13.

* Preheat the oven to 170°C Fan/Gas Mark 5. Grease a 20cm round cake tin and line with non-stick baking paper. Set aside.

* Peel the apples, cut out the core and chop the apples up into 1cm dice.

* In a large mixing bowl, **beat** together the butter and sugar until pale and fluffy.

* Mix in the beaten egg, then **sift** in the flour and **fold** in gently.

* Add the apple, lemon zest and sultanas and stir in evenly. The mixture will be very thick at this stage.

* Pour the mixture into the prepared tin and bake for 30–40 minutes until the cake is risen and golden brown. A skewer or cocktail stick inserted into the centre should come out clean. If it doesn't, return the cake to the oven for a further 5 minutes and then test again.

* Cool in the tin for 20 minutes before turning the cake out and allowing to cool entirely on a wire rack. Sprinkle with the extra tablespoon of caster sugar to serve.

* Store in an airtight container and eat within 3–5 days. Once cool, can be frozen in sealed freezer bags for up to 3 months.

# CHOCOLATE RED WINE CAKE

**Serves: 8–10**

This cake has a texture that is dense and chocolatey, yet light at the same time. It manages to taste of chocolate, fruit and spice all at once, and is a good way to use up leftover wine. It makes an excellent dessert, served with cream, ice cream or crème fraîche, but is equally good with a hot drink at teatime.

Vegetable oil or butter, for greasing

250g butter, softened

250g caster sugar

1 tsp vanilla extract

4 large eggs, beaten

4 tsp cocoa powder

1 tsp cinnamon

Pinch salt

250g self-raising flour

125ml red wine

125g dark chocolate (70% cocoa), melted and cooled (see page 39 for melting instructions)

Icing sugar, for dusting

20cm round cake tin

Non-stick baking paper

For techniques in **bold** see pages 12–13.

* Preheat the oven to 180°C Fan/Gas Mark 6.

* Grease a 20cm round cake tin and line with non-stick baking paper. Set aside.

* In a large mixing bowl, **beat** together the butter and sugar until pale and fluffy.

* Stir the vanilla extract into the beaten egg and then add this to the butter and sugar mixture a little at a time, beating well after every addition.

* **Sift** in the cocoa, cinnamon, salt and self-raising flour. **Fold** gently into the wet mixture.

* Pour in the red wine gradually, mixing well. Finally, pour in the melted chocolate and stir gently to ensure all ingredients are well combined.

* Transfer the mixture to the tin and bake for 45–55 minutes until risen and cooked through. Test this after 45 minutes by inserting a skewer or cocktail stick into the centre. If it comes out clean, the cake is cooked. If some liquid mixture sticks to the cocktail stick, it's not yet ready, so return it to the oven for another 5 minutes and then test again.

* When the cake is cooked, remove from the oven and allow it to cool in the tin for 15 minutes. Then, remove from the tin and leave to cool on a wire rack until fully cool, before dusting with icing sugar to serve.

* Store in an airtight container and eat within 3–5 days. Once cool, slices can be frozen in sealed freezer bags for up to 3 months.

# COFFEE AND WALNUT CAKE

Serves: 8

This cake is a classic, and it's always very popular. Instant espresso powder will give you the most intense coffee flavour, but any instant coffee you have in the cupboard will work – just make sure it's nice and strong. For an extra-special finish, decorate with walnut halves or a sprinkling of chopped walnuts.

## For the cake

Vegetable oil or butter, for greasing

225g butter, softened

225g caster sugar

4 large eggs

2 tsp instant coffee powder dissolved in 1 tbsp hot water

40g ground almonds

225g self-raising flour

1 tsp baking powder

75g walnut pieces

## For the icing

200g icing sugar

100g butter, softened

1 tsp instant coffee powder dissolved in 1 tsp hot water

Walnut halves, pieces or chopped walnuts, to decorate (optional)

Two 20cm round cake tins

Non-stick baking paper

For techniques in **bold** see pages 12–13.

* Preheat the oven to 170°C Fan/Gas Mark 5. Grease two 20cm round cake tins and line with non-stick baking paper. Set aside.

* In a large bowl, **beat** together the butter and sugar until pale and fluffy.

* In a separate bowl, **whisk** the eggs. Add them to the butter and sugar mixture a little at a time. Beat well after every addition.

* Add the coffee and beat vigorously. Then add the ground almonds and stir in well.

* **Sift** in the flour and baking powder, and **fold** in gently. Finally, add the walnut pieces and gently stir in.

* Pour the mixture evenly into the two tins and bake for 25–30 minutes until the cakes are risen and browned. A skewer or cocktail stick inserted into the centre of each should come out clean. If it doesn't, return the cakes to the oven for a further 3 minutes and then test again.

* Meanwhile, make the icing. Sift the icing sugar into a large mixing bowl. Add the butter and coffee and beat the mixture together vigorously until the frosting is very smooth and evenly mixed.

* When the cakes are cooked, leave them to cool in their tins for 20 minutes, before removing and placing on a wire rack until completely cold.

* When the cakes are fully cooled, spread half the icing on top of one cake as the filling, top with the second sponge and spread the remaining icing on top of the cake evenly. Decorate with walnuts, if you like.

* Store in an airtight container and eat within 3–5 days. If iced, store in the fridge. Once cool, can be frozen un-iced in sealed freezer bags for up to 3 months.

# CARAMEL CAKE

Serves: 6–8

This is a delicious light sponge cake sandwiched together and topped with canned caramel, which can be found in the supermarket alongside condensed milk and longlife milk. It's a must for anyone who likes their treats nice and sweet.

Vegetable oil or butter,
for greasing

300g butter, softened

190g dark brown soft sugar

4 medium eggs

600g canned caramel

2 tbsp milk

325g self-raising flour

1 tsp baking powder

Two 20cm round cake tins

Non-stick baking paper

For techniques in **bold**
see pages 12–13.

* Preheat the oven to 170°C Fan/Gas Mark 5. Grease two 20cm round cake tins and line with non-stick baking paper. Set aside.

* In a mixing bowl, **beat** together the butter and sugar until pale and fluffy.

* In a separate bowl, **whisk** the eggs and then pour them a little at a time into the butter and sugar mixture. Beat well after every addition until all the egg is combined.

* Next, add the canned caramel and milk and mix in well. **Sift** in the flour and baking powder and **fold** in lightly.

* Pour the mixture into the prepared tins and bake for 25–30 minutes until the cakes are risen and browned. Test to check if they're cooked by inserting a skewer or cocktail stick into the centre of each. If it comes out clean, the cakes are done. If not, return them to the oven for another 3 minutes and then test again.

* Leave the cakes to cool in the tins for 30 minutes before removing and leaving to cool fully on a wire rack.

* When the cakes are cooled, spread half the canned caramel on top of one cake, place the second cake on top, and spread the remaining canned caramel on top of the second cake to finish. Store in the fridge until you're ready to serve.

* Store in an airtight container and eat within 3–5 days. If iced, store in the fridge. Once cool, can be frozen un-iced in sealed freezer bags for up to 3 months.

# APPLE CIDER CAKE

**Serves: 8–10**

This is a simple-to-make spiced apple cake with juicy pieces of fruit in every slice. The cider makes it really moist, and intensifies the apple flavour – and you can always enjoy a glass while the cake is baking. Use some generously sized eating apples here – any variety you like, but not those large tart cooking apples.

Vegetable oil or butter, for greasing

150g butter, softened

150g caster sugar

2 medium eggs, beaten

200g self-raising flour

Pinch of salt

1 tsp baking powder

1 tsp ground cinnamon

1 tsp mixed spice

150ml good-quality dry cider

4 eating apples, peeled, cored and cut into 5mm-thin slices

4 tbsp demerara sugar

20cm round cake tin

Non-stick baking paper

For techniques in **bold** see pages 12–13.

* Preheat the oven to 170°C Fan/Gas Mark 5. Grease a 20cm round cake tin and line with non-stick baking paper. Set aside.

* In a large mixing bowl, **beat** together the butter and sugar until pale and fluffy.

* Add the beaten eggs, a little at a time, and beat well after each addition.

* **Sift** in the flour, salt, baking powder, cinnamon and mixed spice and gently **fold** in.

* Slowly pour in the cider and stir into the cake batter. Add the eating apples and fold in.

* Pour the cake mixture into the prepared tin, sprinkle with the demerara sugar and bake for 50–60 minutes until the cake is risen and golden brown. A skewer or cocktail stick inserted into the centre of the cake should come out clean. If it doesn't, return the cake to the oven for a further 5 minutes and then test again.

* Cool in the tin for 20 minutes before turning out and allowing to cool fully on a wire rack.

* Store in an airtight container and eat within 3–5 days. Once cool, can be frozen in sealed freezer bags for up to 3 months.

# CARROT CAKE WITH CREAM CHEESE FROSTING

Serves: 8–10

If you asked people what their favourite cake was, carrot cake might just come out top. This cake is loved by everyone who tries it and has the added bonus of being pretty easy and cheap to make.

Vegetable oil or butter,
for greasing

175g dark brown soft sugar

2 large eggs

150ml sunflower oil

200g self-raising flour

2 tsp mixed spice

2 tsp ground cinnamon

1 tsp bicarbonate of soda

Grated zest of 1 orange

200g peeled and grated carrots

110g sultanas

50g desiccated coconut

Cream Cheese Frosting
(page 38)

20cm round cake tin

Non-stick baking paper

For techniques in **bold**
see pages 12–13.

* Preheat the oven to 170°C Fan/Gas Mark 5. Grease a 20cm round cake tin and line with non-stick baking paper. Set aside.

* **Whisk** the sugar, eggs and oil together in a bowl for 2–3 minutes until pale and bubbly around the edges. Check that there is no sugar left undissolved.

* Now **sift** the flour, mixed spice, cinnamon and bicarbonate of soda into the bowl, then **fold** all this in gently. Add the orange zest, grated carrot, sultanas and coconut, and stir in gently.

* Pour the batter into the prepared cake tin and bake for 35–45 minutes until a skewer or cocktail stick inserted into the centre comes out clean. If it does not come out clean, return the cake to the oven for a further 5 minutes and then test again.

* Allow the cake to cool in the tin for 20 minutes before turning out and letting it cool fully on a wire rack. Once completely cold, top with the Cream Cheese Frosting (page 38). Store in the fridge until you want to serve.

* Store in an airtight container and eat within 3–5 days. If iced, store in the fridge. Once cool, can be frozen un-iced in sealed freezer bags for up to 3 months.

# PEACH UPSIDE DOWN CAKE

**Serves: 6–8**

This gorgeous retro cake combines juicy peaches with delicious almondy sponge. Get creative with the peaches and arrange them in whatever pattern you fancy. It's such a simple cake to make, but you're sure to impress!

Vegetable oil or butter,
for greasing

2 tbsp light brown soft sugar

2 peaches, peeled, halved
and stone removed

200g butter, softened

200g caster sugar

3 large eggs

2 tsp vanilla extract

200g ground almonds

Pinch of salt

90g plain flour

20cm round cake tin

Non-stick baking paper

For techniques in **bold**
see pages 12–13.

**Tip:** Canned peaches are fine to use in this recipe. The best ones to buy are peach halves in fruit juice.

* Preheat the oven to 170°C Fan/Gas Mark 5. Grease a 20cm round cake tin and line with non-stick baking paper. Sprinkle the bottom of the tin all over with the brown sugar.

* Cut the peach halves into 1cm thick slices and arrange neatly in concentric circles (or whatever pattern you prefer) in the bottom of the cake tin.

* In a large mixing bowl, **beat** together the butter and sugar until pale and fluffy.

* In a separate bowl, **whisk** the eggs with the vanilla extract. Pour this mixture little by little into the butter and sugar mixture, mixing well after each addition.

* Next, stir in the ground almonds and pinch of salt. **Sift** the flour into the bowl and **fold** in gently.

* Pour the cake mixture carefully over the peaches in the tin and bake for 35–45 minutes until golden and cooked through. Test this by inserting a skewer or cocktail stick into the centre of the cake. If it comes out clean, the cake is cooked. If not, return it to the oven for a further 5 minutes and then test again.

* Leave the cake to cool for 30 minutes in the tin before turning it out upside down onto a wire rack to cool fully. This is also lovely served as a dessert with cream or ice cream.

* Store in an airtight container and eat within 3–5 days. Once cool, can be frozen in sealed freezer bags for up to 3 months.

# BANANA, COCONUT AND CARDAMOM CAKE

**Serves: 12**

This is a light, moist cake with very interesting flavours. Cardamom is an aromatic spice that's used in Indian and Asian cooking. It adds a subtle but intriguing twist to this unusual cake.

Vegetable oil or butter,
for greasing

110g butter, softened

175g caster sugar,
plus extra for sprinkling

1 tsp vanilla extract

2 medium eggs, beaten

475g mashed banana
(approx. 4 large bananas)

150g unsweetened
desiccated coconut

8 cardamom pods,
cut open and seeds
extracted and retained

300g self-raising flour

1 tbsp baking powder

Pinch of salt

20cm round springform tin
Non-stick baking paper

For techniques in **bold**
see pages 12–13.

* Preheat the oven to 180°C Fan/Gas Mark 6. Grease a 20cm round springform cake tin and line with non-stick baking paper. Set aside.

* In a large mixing bowl, **beat** together the butter and sugar until pale and fluffy.

* Add the vanilla extract to the beaten eggs and **whisk** together.

* Pour the egg mixture gradually into the butter and sugar mixture, beating well after every addition.

* Add the mashed banana, coconut and cardamom seeds and mix together until evenly combined.

* Now, **sift** in the flour, baking powder and salt and gently **fold** into the mixture.

* Pour the cake batter into the prepared tin and sprinkle with a handful of caster sugar.

* Bake for 55–65 minutes. Check the cake is cooked by inserting a skewer or cocktail stick into the centre. If it comes out clean, the cake is cooked. If not, return it to the oven for a further 5 minutes and then test again.

* Cool the cake in the tin for 20 minutes before turning out and allowing to cool fully on a wire rack. Sprinkle with caster sugar to decorate.

* Store in an airtight container and eat within 3–5 days. Once cool, can be frozen in sealed freezer bags for up to 3 months.

# GUINNESS CAKE WITH CREAM CHEESE FROSTING

**Serves: 8–10**

This isn't what you might expect from the name, and you don't have to be a Guinness fan to love it – although you will have some Guinness left over, so it helps! The beer makes this sponge light, moist and tangy. Combined with spices and dark sugar, and topped with sweet, creamy frosting, it's a really unusual and memorable cake. The perfect bake for St Patrick's Day!

**Vegetable oil or butter, for greasing**

**200g butter, softened**

**200g dark brown soft sugar**

**4 medium eggs, beaten**

**250g self-raising flour**

**Pinch of salt**

**2 tsp mixed spice**

**165ml Guinness**

**½ quantity of Cream Cheese Frosting (page 38)**

**20cm round springform tin**

**Non-stick baking paper**

For techniques in **bold** see pages 12–13.

* Preheat the oven to 180°C Fan/Gas Mark 6. Grease a 20cm round springform cake tin and line with non-stick baking paper. Set aside.

* In a large mixing bowl, **beat** together the butter and sugar until pale and fluffy.

* Add the beaten eggs, a little at a time, and beat well after each addition.

* **Sift** in the flour, salt and mixed spice, and gently **fold** into the mixture.

* Pour in the Guinness gradually and gently stir in.

* Pour the cake mixture into the prepared cake tin and bake for 40–50 minutes until risen and browned and a skewer or cocktail stick inserted into the centre of the cake comes out clean. If it doesn't, return the cake to the oven for a further 5 minutes and test again.

* Allow the cake to cool for 20 minutes in the tin, then remove and cool fully on a wire rack before adding the frosting to the top of the cake only.

* Store in an airtight container and eat within 3–5 days. If iced, store in the fridge. Once cool, can be frozen un-iced in sealed freezer bags for up to 3 months.

# WHITE RUSSIAN CAKE

**Serves: 10–12**

This gorgeous cake is inspired by the famous White Russian cocktail, but is booze-free so doesn't work out too pricey. With dark, coffee-spiked sponge underneath and a creamy frosting on top, it's still a real treat for parties and celebrations!

### For the cake

Vegetable oil or butter,
for greasing

115g dark chocolate,
broken up into squares

225ml milk

100g butter

250g dark brown soft sugar

100g plain flour

1 tsp baking powder

2 large eggs, beaten

3 tbsp very strong coffee, cooled

### For the topping

150ml double cream

75g full-fat cream cheese

20cm round cake tin
Non-stick baking paper

For techniques in **bold**
see pages 12–13.

* Preheat the oven to 180°C Fan/Gas Mark 6. Grease a 20cm round cake tin and line with non-stick baking paper. Set aside.

* Place the chocolate, milk and butter into a saucepan over a low temperature for around 5 minutes to melt the chocolate and butter. Stir regularly to ensure it doesn't stick or burn.

* Place the sugar, flour and baking powder into a large mixing bowl and stir well to combine the ingredients.

* When the chocolate and butter have melted, **whisk** well to form a smooth, pale-brown liquid. Pour into the mixing bowl and gently stir into the flour and sugar.

* Add the beaten eggs to the mixture and stir in, followed by the coffee.

* The cake mixture will be really liquid, so place the cake tin onto a baking tray as a precaution, and pour the cake batter into the tin.

* Bake for 25–35 minutes until the cake is risen and feels firm and springy to the touch and a skewer or cocktail stick inserted into the centre comes out clean. If it doesn't, return the cake to the oven for a further 5 minutes and then test again. It is a very dense, squidgy cake.

* Allow to cool in the tin for 30 minutes, then remove from the tin and cool fully on a wire rack before adding the topping.

* To make the topping, whisk the cream and cheese together until fluffy, but not too stiff.

* Spread the topping over the top of the cake only.

* Store in an airtight container and eat within 3–5 days. If iced, store in the fridge. Once cool, can be frozen un-iced in sealed freezer bags for up to 3 months.

# PIÑA COLADA CAKE

Serves: 8–10

Here's another fun cocktail-inspired cake – a coconut and pineapple sponge topped with coconut liqueur frosting. Be as inventive as you like when it comes to decorating here. And why not use the rest of the bottle of Malibu as an excuse for throwing a tropical-themed party?

## For the cake

Vegetable oil or butter, for greasing

120g butter, softened

200g caster sugar

3 medium eggs, beaten

1 tbsp Malibu

Pinch of salt

165ml full-fat coconut milk

300g plain flour

1 tsp baking powder

50g desiccated coconut, plus 3 tbsp to decorate

200g crushed pineapple in syrup, drained

100g pineapple slices in syrup, drained and cut into chunks

## For the frosting

115g unsalted butter, softened

500g icing sugar, sifted

2 tbsp coconut milk

2 tsp Malibu

20cm round cake tin

Non-stick baking paper

For techniques in **bold** see pages 12–13.

* Preheat the oven to 170°C Fan/Gas Mark 5. Grease a 20cm round cake tin and line with non-stick baking paper. Set aside.

* In a large mixing bowl, **beat** together the butter and sugar until pale and fluffy.

* Add the beaten eggs a little at a time, mixing well after each addition. Add the Malibu, salt and coconut milk and stir in gently.

* **Sift** in the flour and baking powder and **fold** in gently. Add the desiccated coconut and crushed pineapple, and stir to combine.

* Pour the cake mixture into the prepared tin and bake for 35–45 minutes until risen and browned and a skewer or cocktail stick inserted into the centre comes out clean. If it doesn't, return the cake to the oven for a further 5 minutes and then test again.

* Leave to cool in the tin for 20 minutes before removing and allowing to cool fully on a wire rack before adding frosting.

* To make the frosting, in a large mixing bowl, mix the butter with roughly a third of the icing sugar until thoroughly combined and no longer dry. Gradually add another third of the sugar and mix until well combined. Finally, add the remaining icing sugar and mix in, then beat in the coconut milk and Malibu. Mix well until smooth and creamy.

* Ice the cake and sprinkle with the desiccated coconut. Arrange the pineapple chunks attractively on top of the frosting to decorate.

* Store in an airtight container and eat within 3–5 days. If iced, store in the fridge. Once cool, can be frozen un-iced in sealed freezer bags for up to 3 months.

# CHOCOLATE BIRTHDAY CAKE

**Serves: 8–10**

This is the only recipe you will ever need for chocolate cake! Moist and chocolatey, yet light and fluffy, it's sure to be enjoyed by all. This recipe makes quite a large cake, so there is plenty to share with friends. It's great iced with the Chocolate Fudge Icing (page 39).

Vegetable oil or butter, for greasing

300g butter, softened

500g caster sugar

2 tsp vanilla extract

4 medium eggs, beaten

350g self-raising flour

75g cocoa powder

2 tsp baking powder

125ml milk

125ml boiling water

Chocolate Fudge Icing (page 39)

Two 20cm round cake tins

Non-stick baking paper

For techniques in **bold** see pages 12–13.

* Preheat the oven to 180°C Fan/Gas Mark 6. Grease two 20cm round cake tins and line with non-stick baking paper. Set aside.

* In a large mixing bowl, **beat** together the butter and sugar until pale and fluffy.

* Add the vanilla extract to the beaten eggs and pour into the butter and sugar mixture a little at a time, beating well after each addition.

* **Sift** in the flour, cocoa powder and baking powder, and then **fold** into the mixture gently.

* Add the milk and stir in, followed by the boiling water. Mix well to form a smooth batter.

* Pour the mixture into the prepared cake tins and bake for around 25–35 minutes. Test to see if the cakes are cooked by inserting a skewer or cocktail stick into the centre of each. If it comes out clean, the cake is cooked. If not, return it to the oven for a further 3 minutes and then test again.

* Once the cakes are cooked, cool in the tins for 30 minutes. Then carefully remove from the tins and allow the cakes to cool fully on a wire rack before icing.

* When the cakes are cooled, spread half the Chocolate Fudge Icing (page 39) on top of one cake, place the second cake on top, and spread the remaining icing on the sides and top of the whole cake to finish.

* Store in an airtight container and eat within 3–5 days. If iced, store in the fridge. Once cool, can be frozen un-iced in sealed freezer bags for up to 3 months.

# LOAF CAKES

# FRESH GINGER LOAF CAKE

**Serves: 8**

This cake is seriously good. It's dark and moist, with a sticky top. It's great served with ice cream as a pudding and keeps well too, so is perfect for packed lunches (without the ice cream!).

Vegetable oil or butter, for greasing

230g self-raising flour, sifted

150g dark brown soft sugar

2 tsp ground ginger

½ tsp bicarbonate of soda

Pinch of salt

65g butter, cold and cubed

2.5cm piece of fresh root ginger, peeled and finely grated

2 tbsp treacle

150ml hot water

900g loaf tin

Non-stick baking paper

* Preheat the oven to 180°C Fan/Gas Mark 6. Grease a 900g loaf tin and line with non-stick baking paper.

* Place the flour, sugar, ground ginger, bicarbonate of soda and salt into a large mixing bowl and mix well to combine them together.

* Add the butter and rub it into the flour mixture using your fingertips until the mixture looks like breadcrumbs.

* Add the grated ginger, treacle and hot water and mix until the mixture becomes a smooth batter.

* Pour into the prepared tin and bake for 35–40 minutes until risen and golden brown, and a skewer or cocktail stick inserted into the middle of the cake comes out clean. If it doesn't, return the cake to the oven for another 5 minutes and then test again.

* Allow the cake to cool in the tin for 20 minutes before removing from the tin and leaving it to cool fully on a wire rack.

* Store in an airtight container and eat within 3–5 days. Once cool, can be frozen in sealed freezer bags for up to 3 months.

**Tip:** This recipe is easy to adapt for vegans. Just use a dairy-free spread instead of butter.

# COCONUT AND LIME LOAF CAKE

**Serves: 8**

This dense, moist cake has the subtle flavour and texture of coconut combined with a zesty kick from the fresh limes. It's simple to make but tastes incredible.

Vegetable oil or butter, for greasing

250g butter, softened

250g caster sugar

1 tsp vanilla extract

3 medium eggs, beaten

65g desiccated coconut

Zest and juice of 2 limes (approximately 70ml juice)

250g self-raising flour

2 tsp baking powder

Pinch of salt

900g loaf tin

Non-stick baking paper

For techniques in **bold** see pages 12–13.

* Preheat the oven to 170°C Fan/Gas Mark 5. Grease a 900g loaf tin and line with non-stick baking paper.

* In a large mixing bowl, **beat** together the butter and sugar until pale and fluffy.

* Add the vanilla extract to the beaten egg. **Whisk** well and then add to the butter and sugar mixture a little at a time. Beat well after every addition.

* Next, add the coconut, lime juice and zest and beat well. The mixture will be very liquid at this point.

* **Sift** in the flour, baking powder and salt and gently **fold** into the mixture.

* Pour the batter into the tin and bake for 50–60 minutes until risen and golden brown. Check the cake is cooked by inserting a skewer or cocktail stick into the centre. If it comes out clean, the cake is ready. If not, return it to the oven for a further 5 minutes and then test again.

* Allow the cake to cool for 20 minutes in the tin before removing, as it may be a little fragile. Once removed from the tin, allow to cool fully on a wire rack.

* If you want to ice the cake, see the Tip.

* Store in an airtight container and eat within 3–5 days. Once cool, can be frozen in sealed freezer bags for up to 3 months.

**Tip:** This cake is lovely topped with a lime water icing. Follow the Simple Lemon Water Icing recipe (page 40), replacing the lemon juice with lime juice. Ensure the cake is fully cooled before icing.

# LEMON AND POPPY SEED LOAF CAKE

Serves: 8

This lovely zesty cake is ideal for beginner bakers as it's super-easy to make. The recipe produces a beautifully golden loaf, with a rich yellow sponge speckled with crunchy poppy seeds. It's great topped with the Simple Lemon Water Icing (page 40).

Vegetable oil or butter, for greasing

175g caster sugar

100g butter, softened

Finely grated zest of 2 unwaxed lemons

2 medium eggs

175g self-raising flour

1 tbsp poppy seeds

Pinch of salt

120ml milk

Simple Lemon Water Icing, if using (page 40)

900g loaf tin

Non-stick baking paper

For techniques in **bold** see pages 12–13.

* Preheat the oven to 170°C Fan/Gas Mark 5. Grease a 900g loaf tin and line with non-stick baking paper.

* In a large mixing bowl, **beat** together the sugar, butter and lemon zest until well combined and pale and fluffy.

* Add the eggs and beat vigorously into the mixture.

* **Sift** the flour into the bowl, add the poppy seeds and salt and gently **fold** in.

* Add the milk and lightly stir in.

* Pour the mixture into the tin and bake for 35–45 minutes until the cake is risen and golden brown. Test if the cake is done by inserting a skewer or cocktail stick into the centre. If the cocktail stick comes out clean, the cake is ready. If not, return it to the oven for a further 5 minutes and then test again.

* Leave the cake to cool in the tin for 20 minutes, then turn out and allow to cool fully on a wire rack. If you are icing the cake, make sure it has thoroughly cooled first.

* To ice, pour the Simple Lemon Water Icing (page 40) over the cake and allow to set.

* Store in an airtight container and eat within 3–5 days. If iced, store in the fridge. Once cool, can be frozen un-iced in sealed freezer bags for up to 3 months.

# MARBLE LOAF CAKE

Serves: 8

This loaf cake looks really stunning, with gorgeous swirls of chocolate and vanilla sponge. You don't need to be an artist or even an expert baker to get it right – the method is very simple and anyone can do it.

Vegetable oil or butter,
for greasing
200g butter, softened
200g caster sugar
3 large eggs
200g self-raising flour
1 tsp baking powder
1 tsp vanilla extract
2 tbsp cocoa powder

900g loaf tin
Non-stick baking paper

For techniques in **bold**
see pages 12–13.

* Preheat the oven to 170°C Fan/Gas Mark 5. Grease a 900g loaf tin and line with non-stick baking paper.

* In a large mixing bowl, **beat** together the butter and sugar until pale and fluffy.

* In a separate bowl, **whisk** the eggs. Add them to the butter and sugar a little at a time, and beat well after each addition until the cake batter is smooth and all the egg is mixed in.

* **Sift** in the flour and baking powder and **fold** in gently.

* Transfer half the cake batter to a second mixing bowl, add the vanilla extract to this bowl and stir in gently.

* Sift the cocoa powder into the original bowl of mixture and fold in gently.

* Gently tip the vanilla mixture into the cocoa mixture and stir just a couple of times very gently to swirl the two flavours together. Don't mix too much otherwise the mixture will just turn completely brown.

* Pour the cake batter into the prepared tin and use a knife or a cocktail stick to swirl the mixture further if needed.

* Bake for 40–50 minutes until golden brown. Test the centre with a skewer or cocktail stick. It should come out clean if the cake is cooked. If not, return it to the oven for another 5 minutes and then test again.

* Leave the cake to cool in the tin for 20 minutes, before removing from the tin and leaving to cool fully on a wire rack.

* Store in an airtight container and eat within 3–5 days. Once cool, can be frozen in sealed freezer bags for up to 3 months.

# CHERRY AND ALMOND LOAF CAKE

Serves: 8

This is a dense, buttery loaf cake, dotted with colourful glacé cherries. It's simple to make, yet very special.

Vegetable oil or butter, for greasing
150g butter, softened
150g caster sugar
3 large eggs, beaten
75g ground almonds
150g self-raising flour
1 tsp baking powder
200g glacé cherries

900g loaf tin
Non-stick baking paper

For techniques in **bold** see pages 12–13.

* Preheat the oven to 170°C Fan/Gas Mark 5. Grease a 900g loaf tin and line with non-stick baking paper.

* In a large mixing bowl, **beat** together the butter and sugar until pale and fluffy.

* Beat in the eggs a little bit at a time.

* Stir in the ground almonds. **Sift** in the flour and baking powder and **fold** in gently.

* Add the glacé cherries and stir in so they are evenly distributed.

* Pour the cake mixture into the prepared tin and bake for 45–55 minutes until risen and golden brown, and a skewer or cocktail stick inserted into the centre comes out clean. If it doesn't, return the cake to the oven for another 5 minutes and then test again.

* Allow the cake to cool in the tin for 20 minutes before turning out onto a wire rack to cool fully.

* Store in an airtight container and eat within 3–5 days. Once cool, can be frozen in sealed freezer bags for up to 3 months.

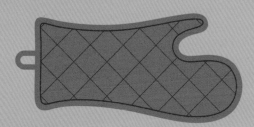

# BANANA AND CHOCOLATE CHIP LOAF CAKE

Serves: 8

This loaf cake is a great way to use up any bananas that are too ripe to eat. The chocolate chips turn it into an indulgent treat.

Vegetable oil or butter, for greasing

250g very ripe bananas (approx. 2 large ones)

2 large eggs

250g caster sugar

1 tsp vanilla extract

50g butter, very soft

250g self-raising flour

1 tsp bicarbonate of soda

150g dark chocolate chips or chopped dark chocolate

900g loaf tin

Non-stick baking paper

For techniques in **bold** see pages 12–13.

* Preheat the oven to 180°C Fan/Gas Mark 6.

* Grease a 900g loaf tin and line with non-stick baking paper.

* In a bowl, mash the bananas well. **Whisk** in the eggs, sugar and vanilla extract.

* Add the butter and **beat** in vigorously until the ingredients are well combined.

* **Sift** in the flour and bicarbonate of soda and **fold** in gently.

* Finally, gently fold in the chocolate chips or chunks.

* Transfer the mixture into the prepared tin and bake for 45 minutes–1 hour until risen and golden brown, and a skewer or cocktail stick inserted into the centre comes out clean. If it doesn't, return the cake to the oven for another 5 minutes and then test again.

* Leave to cool in the tin for 20 minutes before turning out and allowing to cool fully on a wire rack.

* Store in an airtight container and eat within 3–5 days. Once cool, can be frozen in sealed freezer bags for up to 3 months.

**Tip:** When using chocolate chips, it can often work out better value to buy bar of good-quality chocolate and chop it up into small chunks. Bars tend to be better quality than chips and you get more more for your money.

# CHOCOLATE AND ORANGE LOAF CAKE

**Serves: 8**

Chocolate and orange are two flavours made to go together. This cake is moist and intensely zesty, as the whole of the orange is used in the cake – skin and all. Choose either dark or milk chocolate chips, whichever you like best.

Vegetable oil or butter, for greasing

1 large orange

125g butter, softened

175g caster sugar

2 large eggs

1 tsp vanilla extract

250g self-raising flour

1 tsp bicarbonate of soda

175g chocolate chips

150ml water

900g loaf tin

Non-stick baking paper

For techniques in **bold** see pages 12–13.

* Preheat the oven to 170°C Fan/Gas Mark 5. Grease a 900g loaf tin and line with non-stick baking paper.

* Remove the stalk from the orange if it has one and cut it into eighths. Chop each eighth as finely as you can, one piece at a time, retaining all the juice. Make sure you use a good, sharp knife. If you have a food processor, use it to chop the orange, as it will be much quicker than doing it by hand. Place the chopped orange and all the juice in a bowl, and set aside.

* In a mixing bowl, **beat** together the butter and sugar until pale and fluffy.

* In a separate bowl, **whisk** the eggs with the vanilla extract and then pour a little at a time into the sugar and butter. Beat well after every addition until all the egg is all combined.

* **Sift** in the flour and bicarbonate of soda and **fold** in lightly.

* Add the chopped orange and chocolate chips and fold these in lightly too. Finally, add the water and stir in.

* Pour the mixture into the prepared tin and bake for 45–55 minutes until the cake is risen and golden brown. Test to check if it's cooked by inserting a skewer or cocktail stick into the centre. If it comes out clean, the cake is ready. If not, return it to the oven for another 5 minutes and then test again.

* Leave the cake to cool for 20 minutes in the tin before removing and leaving to cool fully on a wire rack.

* Store in an airtight container and eat within 3–5 days. Once cool, can be frozen in sealed freezer bags for up to 3 months.

# CHOCOLATE RUM LOAF CAKE

Serves: 8

If you prefer your treats not so sweet, then this cake is for you. It's dense, chocolatey and a little bit boozy, perfect for using up rum left over from a party. It also makes a really good dessert, served with a scoop of ice cream.

Vegetable oil or butter,
for greasing

170g butter, softened

165g dark brown soft sugar

1 tsp vanilla extract

3 large eggs, beaten

75g self-raising flour

75g cocoa powder

1 tsp baking powder

Pinch of salt

75g ground almonds

4 tbsp rum

4 tbsp milk

900g loaf tin

Non-stick baking paper

For techniques in **bold**
see pages 12–13.

* Preheat the oven to 170°C Fan/Gas Mark 5. Grease a 900g loaf tin and line with non-stick baking paper.

* In a large mixing bowl, **beat** together the butter and sugar until pale and fluffy.

* Stir the vanilla extract into the beaten eggs, then add this a little at a time to the butter and sugar mixture, mixing well after each addition.

* **Sift** in the flour, cocoa powder, baking powder and salt and gently **fold** in to the mixture.

* Finally, stir in the ground almonds, rum and milk. Pour the mixture into the prepared loaf tin and bake for 40–50 minutes until well browned and risen. A skewer or cocktail stick inserted into the centre should come out clean. If it doesn't, return the cake to the oven for another 5 minutes and then test again.

* Leave to cool in the tin for 20 minutes before turning out and allowing to cool fully on a wire rack.

* Store in an airtight container and eat within 3–5 days. Once cool, can be frozen in sealed freezer bags for up to 3 months.

**Tip:** This cake works well with both white and dark rum.

# ST CLEMENT'S LOAF

**Serves: 8**

Named after the nursery rhyme because of its orange and lemon flavours, this cake is simple to prepare, and utterly delicious. It keeps well wrapped in foil and is easy to transport, so it's great for packed lunches. If you fancy this cake iced, the Simple Orange Water Icing (page 40) is very nice.

Vegetable oil or butter, for greasing

110g butter, softened

140g caster sugar

2 large eggs

100g ground almonds

Juice and grated zest of 1 orange

Juice and grated zest of 1 lemon

75g plain flour

1 tsp baking powder

Simple Orange Water Icing, if using (page 40)

Flaked almonds, toasted, to decorate

900g loaf tin

Non-stick baking paper

For techniques in **bold** see pages 12–13.

* Preheat the oven to 170°C Fan/Gas Mark 5. Grease a 900g loaf tin and line with non-stick baking paper.

* In a mixing bowl, **beat** together the butter and sugar until pale and fluffy.

* In a separate bowl, **whisk** the eggs. Pour them gradually into the butter and sugar mixture, beating well after each addition, until all of the egg is completely mixed in.

* Next, add the ground almonds and **fold** in gently, followed by the juice and zest of the orange and lemon.

* Finally, **sift** in the flour and baking powder and gently fold in.

* Pour the cake mixture into the tin and bake for 40–45 minutes until risen and golden brown, and a skewer or cocktail stick inserted in the cake comes out clean. If it doesn't, return the cake to the oven for another 5 minutes and then test again.

* Allow the cake to cool in the tin for 20 minutes before turning out onto a wire rack to cool fully. If you intend to ice your cake, make sure it is completely cool before you do so.

* To ice, pour the Simple Orange Water Icing (page 40) over the cake and allow to set. Decorate with toasted flaked almonds, if you feel like going all out.

* Store in an airtight container and eat within 3–5 days. If iced, store in the fridge. Once cool, can be frozen un-iced in sealed freezer bags for up to 3 months.

# COURGETTE BREAD

**Serves: 8**

This is a cake rather than a bread recipe, but it's called 'bread' because it's less sweet than a normal cake. Courgettes might sound weird, but it's a bit like putting carrots or banana in a cake, and they give a mellow sweetness and make it lovely and moist.

Vegetable oil or butter, for greasing

180g butter

220g light brown soft sugar

3 medium eggs, beaten

1 tsp vanilla extract

Pinch of salt

1 tsp ground cinnamon, plus extra for dusting

Pinch of nutmeg

200g courgettes, washed and grated

200g plain flour

1 tsp baking powder

½ quantity of Cream Cheese Frosting, if using (page 38)

900g loaf tin

Non-stick baking paper

For techniques in **bold** see pages 12–13.

* Preheat the oven to 170°C Fan/Gas Mark 5. Grease a 900g loaf tin and line with non-stick baking paper.

* Melt the butter in a small pan over a gentle heat, or in the microwave. If you use the microwave, set it for just 20 seconds at a time so the butter does not burn.

* In a large mixing bowl, **whisk** the sugar, beaten eggs, vanilla extract, salt, cinnamon and nutmeg together.

* Add the grated courgette and melted butter and stir into the mixture.

* **Sift** in the flour and baking powder and **fold** in gently.

* Pour the mixture into the tin and bake for 45–50 minutes until risen and golden brown, and a skewer or cocktail stick inserted into the centre comes out clean. If it doesn't, return the cake to the oven for another 5 minutes and then test again.

* Cool in the tin for 20 minutes before turning out onto a wire rack to cool entirely. Once cooled, you can top the cake with a half quantity of Cream Cheese Frosting (page 38) and a sprinkling of ground cinnamon if you wish.

* Store in an airtight container and eat within 3–5 days. If iced, store in the fridge. Once cool, can be frozen un-iced in sealed freezer bags for up to 3 months.

**Tip:** Squeeze excess water out of the grated courgettes, so that the cake doesn't end up being soggy.

# WHOLEMEAL BANANA BREAD

Serves: 8

As cakes go, this one is quite hearty, so it's brilliant for an energy boost at any time of the day! It's called 'bread' because it is less sweet and more substantial than traditional banana cake. The fruit makes the cake lovely and moist – for the best outcome, use really ripe bananas.

Vegetable oil or butter,
for greasing
125g butter, softened
200g caster sugar
1 tsp vanilla extract
2 large eggs, beaten
300g mashed ripe banana
(approx. 3 small bananas)
250g wholemeal flour
1 tsp bicarbonate of soda
Pinch of salt
70ml milk
½ quantity of Cream Cheese
Frosting, if using (page 38)

900g loaf tin
Non-stick baking paper

For techniques in **bold**
see pages 12–13.

* Preheat the oven to 180°C Fan/Gas Mark 6. Grease and line a 900g loaf tin with non-stick baking paper and set aside.

* In a large mixing bowl, **beat** together the butter and sugar until pale and fluffy.

* **Whisk** the vanilla extract into the beaten eggs, then add to the butter and sugar mixture, little by little, beating well after every addition.

* Next, add the mashed banana and stir in.

* **Sift** in the flour, bicarbonate of soda and salt and **fold** into the mixture gently.

* Pour in the milk and stir to form a thick batter.

* Tip the cake mixture into the prepared tin and bake for 50–60 minutes until risen and golden brown. A skewer or cocktail stick inserted into the centre should come out clean. If it doesn't, return the cake to the oven for another 5 minutes and then test again.

* Leave to cool in the tin for 20 minutes, then remove from the tin and allow to cool fully on a wire rack. Once cooled, you can top the cake with a half quantity of Cream Cheese Frosting (page 38) if you wish.

* Store in an airtight container and eat within 3–5 days. Once cool, can be frozen in sealed freezer bags for up to 3 months.

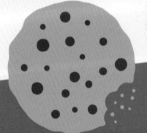

# CHOCOLATE CHIP COOKIES

**Makes: about 15 large cookies**

Soft, chocolatey and slightly chewy, these cookies are amazing eaten fresh from the oven. If you are just learning how to bake, these cookies are a great place to start and will make you very popular with friends and housemates.

**Vegetable oil or butter, for greasing**

**100g butter, softened**

**50g light brown soft sugar**

**50g dark brown soft sugar**

**1 tsp vanilla extract**

**1 large egg, beaten**

**175g self-raising flour**

**200g chocolate chips**

**Two large baking sheets**

**Non-stick baking paper**

For techniques in **bold** see pages 12–13.

* Preheat the oven to 180°C Fan/Gas Mark 6. Grease two large baking sheets well and line with non-stick baking paper.

* In a bowl, **beat** together the butter, both types of sugar and the vanilla extract until pale and fluffy.

* Add the beaten egg to the mixture, a little at a time, and mix until combined.

* **Sift** in the flour and **fold** into the mixture, then add the chocolate chips and stir in.

* Pinch off balls of cookie dough, roughly the size of golf balls, roll them smooth between your hands and place them well spaced apart on the baking sheets.

* Bake the cookies for 8–10 minutes until they are lightly golden.

* Leave to cool on the sheets for 20 minutes before transferring to a wire rack to cool entirely.

* Store in an airtight container and eat within 7 days. Uncooked dough can be frozen in sealed freezer bags for up to 3 months. Bake from frozen (see Tip).

**Tip:** If you don't want to bake all these cookies at once, simply freeze the prepared balls of cookie dough. You can later bake the balls from frozen, allowing a longer cooking time of 11–13 minutes.

# CHOCOLATE ORANGE BISCUITS

**Makes: 12–16 biscuits**

These biscuits are rich, buttery and crumbly, and a great recipe to make when your biscuit tin needs filling up, as they stay fresh for quite a while. The chocolate chips and orange zest make them really special. Perfect for getting you through your revision!

100g butter, softened

100g light brown soft sugar

Finely grated zest
of 1 large orange

1 large egg, beaten

210g plain flour

Pinch of salt

¼ tsp baking powder

50g dark chocolate chips

Vegetable oil or butter,
for greasing

Two large baking sheets

Non-stick baking paper

Round cookie cutter (or glass)

For techniques in **bold**
see pages 12–13.

* In a bowl, **beat** together the butter, sugar and orange zest until pale and fluffy.

* Gradually add the beaten egg, mixing in each addition well.

* **Sift** in the flour, salt and baking powder, mix to combine, then stir in the chocolate chips and bring the mixture together to form a stiff dough.

* Form the dough into a ball and flatten. Wrap in cling film and refrigerate for an hour. Flattening the dough allows it to chill evenly right the way through.

* Meanwhile, preheat the oven to 170°C Fan/Gas Mark 5. Grease two large baking sheets and line with non-stick baking paper.

* Once the dough is chilled, lay out two large sheets of cling film on a clean work surface. Place the dough in the centre of one sheet of cling film and place the second sheet on top. Roll out the dough between the two sheets of cling film until it is only as thick as the chocolate chips. You'll feel the pin rolling against them once you get the dough thin enough.

* Using a cookie cutter or drinking glass, cut out the biscuits and lay them on the prepared baking sheets.

* When you have cut out as many as you can, bring the remaining dough back together to form a ball and roll out again. Repeat until you have used up all the dough.

* Bake the biscuits for 13–15 minutes until they are lightly browned and feel firm to the touch. Leave to cool on the sheets for around 20 minutes before transferring to a wire rack to cool fully.

* Store in an airtight container and eat within 7 days.

# WHITE CHOCOLATE AND CRANBERRY COOKIES

**Makes: about 15 large cookies**

The combination of sweet white chocolate and sharp, chewy cranberries is unbelievably good. These cookies look very pretty too, and are great for sharing.

Vegetable oil or butter,
for greasing

100g butter, softened

50g light brown soft sugar

50g dark brown soft sugar

1 tsp vanilla extract

1 large egg, beaten

175g self-raising flour

100g white chocolate chips

75g dried cranberries

Two large baking sheets

Non-stick baking paper

For techniques in **bold**
see pages 12–13.

* Preheat the oven to 180°C Fan/Gas Mark 6. Grease two large baking sheets well and line with non-stick baking paper.

* In a mixing bowl, **beat** together the butter, both types of sugar and the vanilla extract until pale and fluffy.

* Add the beaten egg a little at a time, mixing in well after each addition, until all the egg has been combined.

* **Sift** in the flour and **fold** into the mixture, then add the chocolate chips and cranberries and stir in.

* Pinch off balls of cookie dough, roughly the size of golf balls, roll them smooth between your hands and place them well spaced apart on the baking sheets.

* Bake the cookies for 8–10 minutes until they are lightly golden.

* Leave to cool on the sheets for 20 minutes, during which time they will firm up, before transferring to a wire rack to cool entirely.

* Store in an airtight container and eat within 7 days. Uncooked dough can be rolled into balls and frozen in sealed freezer bags for up to 3 months. Bake from frozen, adding an extra 2–4 minutes to the cooking time given above.

# CHOCOLATE MARSHMALLOW COOKIES

**Makes: 10–12 cookies**

The marshmallows give a lovely chewiness to these cookies. Make sure you bake them on non-stick paper, as the marshmallows will be quite sticky when they come out of the oven and can get horribly stuck if put directly on a baking sheet. See picture on the next page.

Vegetable oil or butter,
for greasing
55g butter, softened
65g caster sugar
65g dark brown soft sugar
1 large egg, beaten
1 tsp vanilla extract
110g self-raising flour
Pinch of salt
20g cocoa powder
½ tsp baking powder
20g mini marshmallows

Two large baking sheets
Non-stick baking paper

For techniques in **bold**
see pages 12–13.

* Preheat the oven to 180°C Fan/Gas Mark 6. Grease two large baking sheets really well and line with non-stick baking paper. This is important, as these cookies can easily stick.

* In a mixing bowl, **beat** together the butter and both types of sugar until pale and fluffy.

* Mix together the beaten egg and vanilla extract, then add to the butter and sugar mixture a little at a time, stirring vigorously after each addition.

* **Sift** in the flour, salt, cocoa powder and baking powder, and stir in well to form a stiff dough.

* Add the mini marshmallows and stir to distribute evenly.

* Pinch off walnut-sized pieces of dough and roll into smooth balls between your hands. Place well spaced apart on the baking sheets.

* Bake for 9–11 minutes until browned and crisp at the edges and the marshmallows have melted. The cookies will still be soft when you remove them from the oven, but will firm up quickly. Leave them to cool for 20 minutes on the baking sheets before transferring to a wire rack to cool completely.

* Store in an airtight container and eat within 5 days. Once cool, cookies can be frozen in sealed freezer bags for up to 3 months.

# CINNAMON SUGAR COOKIES

**Makes: 16–18 cookies**

These are really simple buttery biscuits, quite like shortbread, but dusted with cinnamon sugar. They keep very well if stored in a sealed container. You'll need to chill your dough for 3 hours before baking, so leave yourself time.

### For the cookie dough
115g butter, softened

200g caster sugar

1 large egg, beaten

1 tsp vanilla extract

250g plain flour

Pinch of salt

Vegetable oil or butter, for greasing

### For dusting the cookies
4 tsp caster sugar

1 tbsp ground cinnamon

Two large baking sheets
Non-stick baking paper

For techniques in **bold** see pages 12–13.

* In a large mixing bowl, **beat** together the butter and sugar until pale and fluffy.

* Combine the egg and vanilla extract, then add gradually to the butter and sugar mixture, beating well after each addition. **Sift** in the flour and salt, and stir well to form a stiff dough.

* Form the cookie dough into a ball and roll into a log shape. Wrap in cling film. Chill for at least 3 hours before using.

* When you are ready to bake your cookies, preheat the oven to 190°C Fan/Gas Mark 6. Grease two large baking sheets and line with non-stick baking paper.

* Unwrap the chilled dough and cut into 16–18 slices.

* Place the extra dusting sugar and cinnamon on a plate and stir together. Toss each slice of dough in the cinnamon sugar.

* Place the slices of dough onto the prepared baking sheets and flatten them if necessary using the ball of your hand. Sprinkle with an extra pinch of cinnamon sugar. Ensure they are very well spaced on the baking sheets as they will spread out significantly when baking.

* Bake the cookies for 12 minutes until pale golden. They will still be soft when you remove them from the oven. Leave to cool on the sheets for 20 minutes before transferring to a wire rack to cool entirely.

* Store in an airtight container and eat within 7 days. Uncooked dough can be sliced and frozen in sealed freezer bags for up to 3 months. Bake from frozen, adding an extra 2–4 minutes to the cooking time given above.

# BANANA AND CHOCOLATE CHIP COOKIES

**Makes: 12–16 large cookies**

These chunky, buttery cookies are moist in the middle and chewy around the edges, with a soft texture and a gorgeous banana taste. The recipe is quite unusual, as it doesn't contain eggs (which also makes it very easy to adapt for vegans – see Tip below).

Vegetable oil or butter, for greasing

90g butter, softened

225g caster sugar

1 large banana, mashed

2 tbsp milk

1 tsp vanilla extract

300g plain flour

2 tsp bicarbonate of soda

Pinch of salt

100g chocolate chips

Two large baking sheets

Non-stick baking paper

For techniques in **bold** see pages 12–13.

* Preheat the oven to 180°C Fan/Gas Mark 6. Grease two large baking sheets and line with non-stick baking paper.

* In a large mixing bowl, **beat** together the butter and sugar until pale and fluffy.

* Add the mashed banana, milk and vanilla extract and beat into the mixture.

* **Sift** in the flour, bicarbonate of soda and salt, and beat in well.

* **Fold** in the chocolate chips.

* Spoon out the mixture into blobs on the baking sheets, well spaced apart.

* Bake the cookies for 10–15 minutes until lightly browned and crisp at the edges. When you remove the cookies from the oven, they will still be soft. Leave them to cool on the sheets for around 20 minutes before transferring to a wire rack to cool fully.

* Store in an airtight container and eat within 5 days. Once cool, these cookies can be frozen in sealed freezer bags for up to 3 months.

**Tip:** To make these cookies vegan, use dairy-free spread, non-dairy milk and vegan chocolate chopped into chunks.

# DOUBLE CHOCOLATE CHUNK COOKIES

**Makes: 10–12 cookies**

*A chocoholic's dream, these cookies are lightly crisp at the edges and chewy in the centre.*

Vegetable oil or butter,
for greasing
55g butter, softened
65g caster sugar
65g dark brown soft sugar
1 large egg, beaten
1 tsp vanilla extract
110g self-raising flour
Pinch of salt
20g cocoa powder
½ tsp baking powder
150g dark chocolate chunks

Two large baking sheets
Non-stick baking paper

For techniques in **bold**
see pages 12–13.

* Preheat the oven to 180°C Fan/Gas Mark 6. Grease two large baking sheets really well and line with non-stick baking paper. This is important as these cookies can easily stick.

* In a mixing bowl, **beat** together the butter and both types of sugar until pale and fluffy.

* Combine the beaten egg and vanilla extract, then gradually add to the mixture, beating vigorously after each addition.

* **Sift** in the flour, salt, cocoa powder and baking powder, and stir well to form a stiff dough.

* Add the chocolate chunks and stir to distribute evenly.

* Pinch off walnut-sized pieces of dough and roll into smooth balls between your hands. Place on the baking sheets well spaced apart.

* Bake for 9–11 minutes until the cookies are crispy at the top and edges and the chocolate chunks have melted. They will still be soft when you remove them from the oven, but will firm up quickly. Leave to cool for 20 minutes on the baking sheets before transferring to a wire rack to cool completely.

* Store in an airtight container and eat within 7 days. Uncooked dough can be rolled into balls and frozen in sealed freezer bags for up to 3 months. Bake from frozen, adding an extra 2–4 minutes to the cooking time given above.

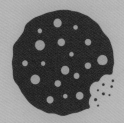

# BLACK FOREST COOKIES

**Makes: 12–16 cookies**

These delicious chewy cookies are totally irresistible – so they won't last long. The name 'Black Forest' traditionally *refers* to a mix of cherries and chocolate, and these are packed full of both.

Vegetable oil or butter, for greasing

80g butter, softened

200g caster sugar

1 medium egg, beaten

1 tsp vanilla extract

165g plain flour

35g cocoa powder

½ tsp baking powder

¼ tsp bicarbonate of soda

90g glacé cherries, halved

60g dark chocolate chips

Two large baking sheets

Non-stick baking paper

For techniques in **bold** see pages 12–13.

* Preheat the oven to 170°C Fan/Gas Mark 5. Grease two large baking sheets and line with non-stick baking paper.

* In a large mixing bowl, **beat** together the butter and sugar until pale and fluffy.

* Add the beaten egg and vanilla extract and beat into the mixture.

* **Sift** in the flour, cocoa powder, baking powder and bicarbonate of soda, and beat in well.

* Now, add the cherries and chocolate chips and stir into the mixture until evenly distributed.

* Form balls of mixture roughly the size of a golf ball and place on the baking sheets, well spaced apart. The mixture will be really sticky, so before handling the dough, briefly run your hands under the cold water tap so they are damp, and then the mixture won't stick to them.

* Bake the cookies for 12 minutes until they are crispy at the top and edges and the chocolate chips have melted. When you remove them from the oven, they will still be soft. Leave on the sheets for around 20 minutes to firm up before transferring to a wire rack to cool fully.

* Store in an airtight container and eat within 7 days. Once cool, these cookies can be frozen in sealed freezer bags for up to 3 months.

# CHEWY OAT AND SULTANA COOKIES

**Makes: 10–12 cookies**

If you prefer to take it easy on the sugar, you'll like these cookies. They have a delicious oaty texture with just a hint of sweetness.

Vegetable oil or butter,
for greasing

110g butter, softened

65g light brown soft sugar

65g caster sugar

1 large egg, beaten

150g porridge oats

85g plain flour, plus
a little extra for dusting

100g sultanas

Large baking sheet
Non-stick baking paper

For techniques in **bold**
see pages 12–13.

* Preheat the oven to 190°C Fan/Gas Mark 6. Grease a large baking sheet and line with non-stick baking paper.

* In a large mixing bowl, **beat** together the butter and both types of sugar until pale and fluffy.

* Next, add the beaten egg a little at a time, stirring well after each addition. Add the oats and stir in.

* Finally, **sift** in the flour, add the sultanas and stir to combine.

* Pinch off walnut-sized pieces of cookie dough and roll into smooth balls between your hands. Place the balls on the prepared baking sheet, set well apart from each other as they will expand when cooking.

* Dust the base of a clean drinking glass with flour. Use this to press down on each cookie to flatten them a little.

* Bake the cookies in the oven for 10–12 minutes until they are lightly browned.

* Leave to cool on the sheet for 20 minutes before transferring to a wire rack to cool fully.

* Store in an airtight container and eat within 5 days. Once cool, these cookies can be frozen in sealed freezer bags for up to 3 months.

# TROPICAL FRUIT COOKIES

**Makes: 12–16 large cookies**

For the fruit in these, a mixture of dried papaya, banana and pineapple is really tasty, but feel free to use any dried fruit you like.

Vegetable oil or butter,
for greasing

100g butter, softened

100g caster sugar

100g light brown soft sugar

1 medium egg, beaten

1 tsp vanilla extract

4 tbsp sunflower oil

200g plain flour

Pinch of salt

½ tsp baking powder

150g dried tropical fruit, e.g.
banana chips, pineapple and
papaya pieces

50g desiccated coconut

Two large baking sheets

Non-stick baking paper

For techniques in **bold**
see pages 12–13.

* Preheat the oven to 170°C Fan/Gas Mark 5. Grease two large baking sheets and line with non-stick baking paper.

* In a mixing bowl, **beat** together the butter and both types of sugar until pale and fluffy.

* Combine the beaten egg and vanilla extract and add this to the butter and sugar mixture a little at a time, stirring well after each addition. Then pour in the sunflower oil and mix well.

* **Sift** in the flour, salt and baking powder. Stir to form a stiff dough.

* Add the dried fruit, banana chips and desiccated coconut and stir to distribute evenly.

* Spoon out the mixture onto the baking sheets, allowing a generous 2 tablespoons of mixture per cookie. Space them well apart on the tray as they spread quite a bit while baking.

* Bake for 8–12 minutes until the cookies are lightly browned. They will still be soft when you remove them from the oven, so allow to cool for 20 minutes on the sheets, during which time they will firm up, then transfer to a wire rack to cool fully.

* Store in an airtight container and eat within 5 days. Once cool, these cookies can be frozen in sealed freezer bags for up to 3 months.

# PEANUT BUTTER BISCUITS

**Makes: 10 biscuits**

Crispier and crunchier than a cookie, these yummy biscuits
also last longer in the biscuit tin (depending on your will power!).
The combination of sweet and salty here is perfect.

Vegetable oil or butter,
for greasing

50g butter, softened

50g caster sugar

1 medium egg, beaten

110g crunchy peanut butter

150g plain flour, plus
extra for dusting

**Large baking sheet**

**Non-stick baking paper**

For techniques in **bold**
see pages 12–13.

* Preheat the oven to 180°C Fan/Gas Mark 6. Grease a large
  baking sheet and line with non-stick baking paper.

* In a mixing bowl, **beat** together the butter and sugar until pale
  and fluffy.

* Pour in the beaten egg a little at a time, mixing after each
  addition. Add the peanut butter and stir through well.

* **Sift** in the flour and then **fold** into the mixture. You should now
  have a stiff dough.

* With your hands, roll the dough into balls the size of walnuts
  and place on the baking sheet, making sure they are well
  spaced apart.

* Dust the base of a clean drinking glass with flour. Use this to
  press down on each biscuit to flatten them.

* Bake the biscuits in the oven for 9–11 minutes until they
  are very lightly browned.

* Leave the biscuits to cool on the sheet for around 20 minutes
  before transferring to a wire rack to cool completely.

* Store in an airtight container and eat within 7 days.

# MELTING MOMENTS

**Makes: 8–10 biscuits**

These are wonderfully retro biscuits, which were very popular in the 1950s. They are light and buttery, like shortbread, and keep very well in an airtight container.

125g butter, softened

75g caster sugar

1 tsp vanilla extract

125g self-raising flour

Vegetable oil or butter, for greasing

3–4 tbsp desiccated coconut

8–10 glacé cherries (one per biscuit)

Large baking sheet

Non-stick baking paper

For techniques in **bold** see pages 12–13.

* In a mixing bowl, **beat** together the butter, sugar and vanilla extract until pale and fluffy.

* **Sift** in the flour and then mix in well. Bring the mixture together to form a dough.

* Wrap the dough in cling film and chill in the fridge for 30 minutes.

* Meanwhile, preheat the oven to 180°C Fan/Gas Mark 6. Grease a large baking sheet and line with non-stick baking paper. Spread the desiccated coconut on a plate.

* Once the dough has chilled, pinch off walnut-sized balls of the mixture, roll in the desiccated coconut and place on the prepared baking sheet.

* Using the bottom of a clean drinking glass, press down on each ball gently to flatten it a little, then place a cherry on top.

* Bake the biscuits for 10–15 minutes until golden.

* Leave to cool on the sheet for 20 minutes before transferring to a wire rack to cool fully.

* Store in an airtight container and eat within 7 days.

# GINGER COOKIES

**Makes: 12 large cookies**

*These are the cookie equivalent of a gingernut, ideal for anyone who loves that spicy ginger hit but prefers their biscuits large, soft and chewy.*

Vegetable oil or butter,
for greasing

165g butter, softened

65g light brown soft sugar

100g caster sugar

1 medium egg, beaten

315g plain flour

Pinch of salt

2 tsp bicarbonate of soda

4 tsp ground ginger

2 tbsp golden syrup

**Two large baking sheets**

**Non-stick baking paper**

For techniques in **bold**
see pages 12–13.

* Preheat the oven to 170°C Fan/Gas Mark 5. Grease two large baking sheets and line with non-stick baking paper.

* In a mixing bowl, **beat** together the butter and both types of sugar until pale and fluffy.

* Add the beaten egg a little at a time, mixing well after each addition.

* **Sift** in the flour, salt, bicarbonate of soda and ground ginger, and stir well to form a stiff dough.

* Add the golden syrup and stir into the mixture.

* Spoon out the mixture onto the baking sheets, spacing the cookies well apart. You want a generous 2 tablespoons of mixture per cookie.

* Bake for 10–12 minutes until the cookies are lightly browned. They will still be soft when you remove them from the oven, so allow to cool for 20 minutes on the sheets, during which time they will firm up, and then transfer onto a wire rack to cool fully.

* Store in an airtight container and eat within 7 days. Once cool, these cookies can be frozen in sealed freezer bags for up to 3 months.

# OATMEAL AND TOFFEE COOKIES

**Makes: 12 large cookies**

*This combination of soft oatiness and chewy toffee chunks is totally irresistible. These cookies are ideal if you need an energy boost.*

Vegetable oil or butter,
for greasing

140g butter, softened

120g light brown soft sugar

150g caster sugar

1 medium egg, beaten

1 tsp vanilla extract

200g oatmeal

240g plain flour

1 tsp bicarbonate of soda

12 toffees, chopped

**Two large baking sheets**
**Non-stick baking paper**

For techniques in **bold**
see pages 12–13.

* Preheat the oven to 180°C Fan/Gas Mark 6. Grease two large baking sheets and line with non-stick baking paper.

* In a large mixing bowl, **beat** together the butter and both types of sugar until pale and fluffy.

* Combine the beaten egg and vanilla extract, then add to the mixture a little at a time, beating well after each addition.

* Add the oatmeal to the mixture and **sift** in the flour and bicarbonate of soda. Stir into the mixture.

* Now add the chopped toffees and stir again.

* Spoon out dollops of mixture onto the prepared baking sheets, each about 1 tablespoon, ensuring they are well spaced apart.

* Bake for 8–12 minutes until lightly golden brown.

* Allow to cool on the sheets for 10 minutes, then transfer to a wire rack to cool completely. Do not eat until cool as the toffees will be extremely hot.

* Store in an airtight container and eat within 5 days. Once cool, these cookies can be frozen in sealed freezer bags for up to 3 months.

# CARAMEL SANDWICH COOKIES

**Makes: 12 sandwich cookies**

Canned caramel can be found in UK supermarkets near the condensed milk. In this recipe it's sandwiched between two pieces of shortbread. Be warned, these are seriously addictive!

Vegetable oil or butter,
for greasing
125g butter, softened
50g caster sugar
175g plain flour
6 tbsp canned caramel
Icing sugar, for sprinkling

Large baking sheet
Non-stick baking paper
Rolling pin (or wine bottle)
Round cookie cutter (or glass)

For techniques in **bold**
see pages 12–13.

* Preheat the oven to 150°C Fan/Gas Mark 3. Grease a large baking sheet and line with non-stick baking paper.

* In a large mixing bowl, **beat** together the butter and sugar until pale and fluffy. **Sift** in the flour and mix to a stiff dough.

* Turn the dough out onto a large sheet of cling film. Bring the dough together to form a ball. Place a second large sheet of cling film over the dough.

* With a rolling pin or clean wine bottle, roll out the dough between the cling film sheets to roughly 1cm in thickness, then peel back the top layer of cling film and cut out small discs using a cookie cutter or clean drinking glass. Place the discs onto the prepared baking sheet, well spaced apart.

* When you have cut out as many discs as you can, bring the remaining dough together into a ball again. Replace the top layer of cling film, roll out again and then cut out more cookies. Repeat until all the dough has been used up. You need 24 small discs in total.

* Bake the cookies for 18–20 minutes until very lightly browned. They will turn dark brown very quickly, so do check after 18 minutes, and check every minute or so from then on if they're not yet done.

* Allow the cookies to cool for 10 minutes on the sheet then transfer to a wire rack to cool fully.

* When the cookies are cold, place about 1 teaspoon of canned caramel onto one cookie then sandwich a second cookie on top. Repeat, so that you have 12 sandwiched cookies in total. Sprinkle with icing sugar and enjoy!

* Store in an airtight container and eat within 2–3 days.

# SHORTBREAD

**Makes: 10–15 biscuits (depending on cutter size)**

Homemade shortbread is so easy to make! It's delicious served with ice cream, and also makes a great gift, as it keeps well in an airtight container. Rolling the dough between two sheets of cling film helps make the perfect biscuit every time.

Vegetable oil or butter, for greasing

**125g butter, softened**

**50g caster sugar, plus extra for sprinkling**

**175g plain flour**

**Large baking sheet**

**Non-stick baking paper**

**Rolling pin (or wine bottle)**

**Cookie cutters (or a glass)**

For techniques in **bold** see pages 12–13.

* Preheat the oven to 150°C Fan/Gas Mark 3. Grease a large baking sheet and line with non-stick baking paper.

* In a large mixing bowl, **beat** together the butter and sugar until pale and fluffy.

* **Sift** in the flour and mix to form a stiff dough.

* Turn the shortbread dough out onto a large sheet of cling film. Bring the dough together to form a ball.

* Place a second large sheet of cling film over the dough.

* With a rolling pin or clean wine bottle, roll out the dough between the cling film sheets to roughly 1cm in thickness, then peel back the top layer of cling film and start to cut out biscuits using a cookie cutter or small drinking glass.

* Place the shortbread shapes on the prepared baking sheet.

* When you have cut out as many biscuits as you can from the dough, bring the offcuts together into a ball again. Replace the top layer of cling film, roll out again and cut more biscuits. Repeat until all the dough has been used up.

* Bake the shortbread for 18–25 minutes until it is very lightly browned. The shortbread will turn dark brown very quickly, so do check it after 18 minutes, and check every minute or so from then on if it's not yet done.

* Allow the biscuits to cool on a wire rack for 10 minutes, then sprinkle them with caster sugar and transfer to a wire rack to cool fully.

* Store in an airtight container and eat within 14 days.

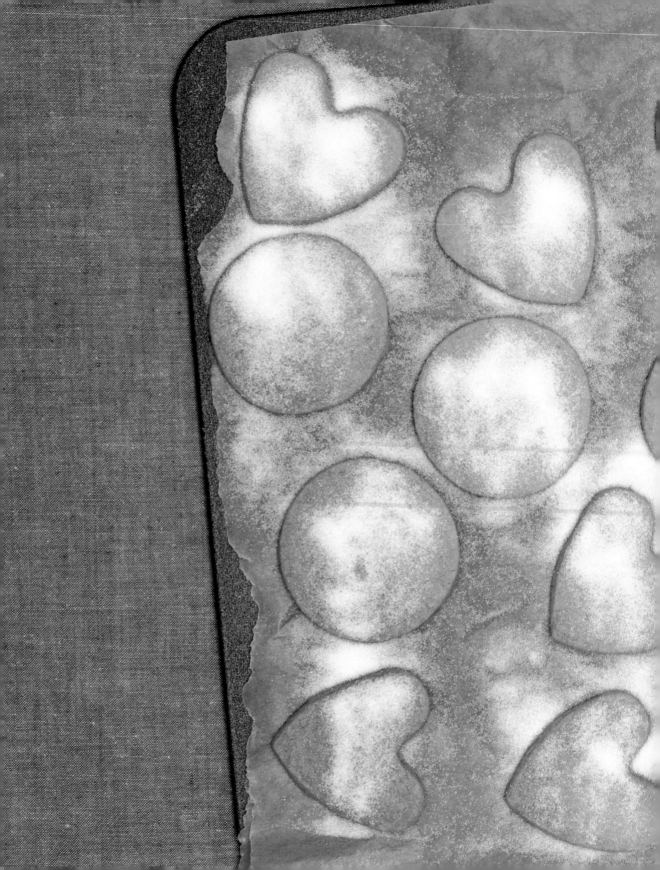

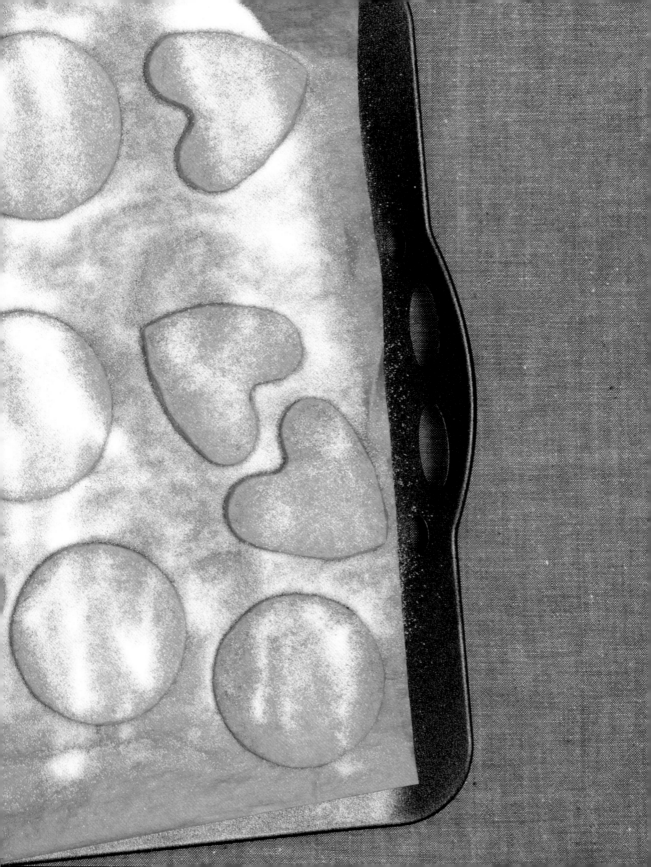

TRAYBAKES

# CHOCOLATE FUDGE BROWNIES

**Makes: 12–14 brownies**

Dark, dense and squidgy, these brownies are a real treat. They taste
even better a day or two after baking so can be made in advance if
you like. Use the best-quality chocolate you can afford – it makes all
the difference to the finished brownies.

Vegetable oil or butter,
for greasing

190g dark chocolate,
broken into squares

125g salted butter

1 tsp instant coffee powder

250g caster sugar

3 large eggs, beaten

60g self-raising flour

1 tsp cocoa powder

20cm square cake tin

Non-stick baking paper

For techniques in **bold**
see pages 12–13.

**Tip:** Make an incredible
ice cream sundae by
piling ice cream on top of
these brownies. Drizzle
with melted chocolate
and, if you want to go all
out, add whipped cream
and chopped nuts too.

* Preheat the oven to 180°C Fan/Gas Mark 6. Grease a 20cm
  square cake tin and line with non-stick baking paper.

* Melt the chocolate and butter together. You can do this in the
  microwave (make sure you check it every 20 seconds so that
  it does not burn) or in a heatproof bowl over a small saucepan
  of simmering water (stir frequently and check the water isn't
  actually in contact with the bottom of the bowl).

* When the chocolate and butter are melted, mix vigorously to
  combine the two. Add the coffee powder, stir again and leave
  to cool for 10 minutes or so.

* Add the sugar to the chocolate mixture once it has cooled
  a little, followed by the eggs.

* **Sift** in the flour and cocoa powder and gently **fold** in.

* Pour the mixture into the prepared tin and bake in the oven
  for 35–40 minutes until the top has a shiny crust. Be careful
  not to overcook, as the brownies will solidify as they cool –
  but you want them to stay nice and fudgy in the middle.

* Allow to cool completely in the tin before slicing up.
  (When slicing, cut carefully so as not to scratch the tin.)

* Store in an airtight container and eat within 7 days.

# PEANUT BLONDIES

**Makes: 12 slices**

Blondies are basically white-chocolate brownies, and these are made with a combination of sweet white chocolate and salty peanut butter. They are incredibly delicious and dangerously addictive!

Vegetable oil or butter, for greasing

100g white chocolate, broken into squares

60g butter, softened

100g caster sugar

150g light brown soft sugar

2 medium eggs, beaten

1 tsp vanilla extract

150g peanut butter (crunchy works well here, but smooth is fine)

80g plain flour

¼ tsp baking powder

Pinch of salt

20cm square cake tin

Non-stick baking paper

For techniques in **bold** see pages 12–13.

* Preheat the oven to 180°C Fan/Gas Mark 6. Grease a 20cm square cake tin and line with non-stick baking paper.

* Melt the chocolate. You can do this in a non-metallic bowl in the microwave (check it every 20 seconds to ensure it does not burn) or in a heatproof bowl over a small saucepan of simmering water (stir frequently and check the water isn't actually in contact with the bottom of the bowl).

* When the chocolate is melted, set aside and allow to cool for 10 minutes or so.

* In a mixing bowl, **beat** together the butter and both types of sugar until pale and fluffy.

* Combine the beaten eggs and vanilla extract and add to the mixture along with the peanut butter. Beat in vigorously until well mixed.

* Pour in the cooled melted chocolate and stir to combine well.

* **Sift** in the flour, baking powder and salt, and **fold** in.

* Pour the mixture into the tin and bake for 25–35 minutes. Be careful not to overcook or the blondies will be dry.

* Allow to cool fully in the tin before cutting into slices. (Cut them carefully so as not to scratch the tin.)

* Store in an airtight container and eat within 7 days.

# PEACH MELBA SQUARES

**Makes: 9 squares**

These are named after a famous American dessert which combines peaches and raspberries. The two fruits are delicious baked together in a vanilla sponge, which looks and tastes gorgeous cut into squares and served with a dusting of icing sugar.

Vegetable oil or butter,
for greasing

165g butter, softened

200g caster sugar

1 tsp vanilla extract

2 large eggs

135g self-raising flour

35g ground almonds

2 ripe peaches

150g raspberries

Icing sugar, for dusting

20cm square cake tin

Non-stick baking paper

For techniques in **bold**
see pages 12–13.

> **Tip:** Canned peaches work fine here – just make sure you drain them well first. It's also a good way to use up raspberries that have become too squidgy to eat. Or use frozen raspberries (defrosted and excess juice discarded).

* Preheat the oven to 180°C Fan/Gas Mark 6. Grease a 20cm square cake tin and line with non-stick baking paper.

* In a large mixing bowl, **beat** together the butter and sugar until pale and fluffy.

* Place the vanilla extract in a small bowl, add the eggs and **whisk** together. Add this mixture to the butter and sugar a little at a time, beating well after each addition.

* **Sift** in the flour and **fold** in, then add the ground almonds and stir in gently.

* Cut the peaches in half and remove the skin. Cut into 1cm chunks, and tip into the cake batter along with the raspberries. Stir in gently.

* Gently tip the cake mixture into the prepared tin and smooth the top.

* Bake for around 40 minutes until a skewer or cocktail stick inserted into the centre comes out clean. If it doesn't, return the cake to the oven for another 3 minutes and then test again.

* Leave to cool in the tin for at least 20 minutes before removing and placing on a wire rack to cool fully. Cut into squares once cool. Dust with icing sugar.

* Store in an airtight container and eat within 7 days.

# CAPPUCCINO SLICES

**Makes: 12 slices**

These yummy squares have coffee-flavoured sponge and a delicious creamy topping. The coffee flavour here is subtle rather than overwhelming, and a dusting of cocoa or chocolate is the perfect finishing touch. Why not serve with coffee?

**For the cake base**

Vegetable oil or butter, for greasing

225g butter, softened

225g light brown soft sugar

3 medium eggs, beaten

275g self-raising flour

35g ground almonds

1 tbsp instant coffee powder dissolved in 1 tbsp hot water

**For the topping**

250g mascarpone cheese

2 tsp light brown soft sugar

2 tbsp cocoa powder or drinking chocolate, for dusting

20cm square cake tin

Non-stick baking paper

For techniques in **bold** see pages 12–13.

* Preheat the oven to 180°C Fan/Gas Mark 6. Grease a 20cm square cake tin and line with non-stick baking paper.

* In a mixing bowl, **beat** together the butter and sugar until pale and fluffy.

* Add the eggs and beat into the mixture.

* **Sift** in the flour and **fold** in gently, followed by the ground almonds and coffee.

* When all the ingredients are evenly combined, pour into the prepared tin and bake for 30–35 minutes. Test to see if the cake is cooked by inserting a skewer or cocktail stick into the centre. If it comes out clean, the cake is cooked. If not, return it to the oven for a further 5 minutes and then test again.

* Turn the cake out of the tin and allow to cool fully on a wire rack.

* When the cake is cooled, you can make the topping. Simply beat together the mascarpone cheese and sugar and spread evenly over the top of the cake.

* Dust with cocoa powder or drinking chocolate and slice up.

* Store in an airtight container in the fridge. Eat within 2 days.

# GINGER PARKIN

**Makes: approximately 9 large squares**

This is a simple, traditional recipe from the north of England, made with oatmeal and treacle. It is particularly delicious when left in an airtight container for a week or even two after being baked, so it's ideal for making in advance to get you through your exams.

Vegetable oil or butter, for greasing

80g butter

85g dark brown soft sugar

6 tbsp golden syrup

1 tbsp treacle

75g self-raising flour

1 tbsp ground ginger

Pinch of salt

175g oatmeal

1 medium egg, beaten

20cm square cake tin

Non-stick baking paper

For techniques in **bold** see pages 12–13.

* Preheat the oven to 150°C Fan/Gas Mark 3. Grease a 20cm square cake tin and line with non-stick baking paper.

* Place the butter, sugar, golden syrup and treacle in a small saucepan and heat gently over a low heat until the butter has melted. Mix to combine the ingredients.

* **Sift** the flour, ginger and salt into a large bowl, add the oatmeal and mix to combine evenly.

* Pour the warm mixture from the saucepan into the oatmeal mixture and gently stir in.

* Next, add the beaten egg and mix.

* Gently pour the mixture into the prepared tin and bake for 35–45 minutes until the parkin is golden brown and the centre of the cake feels springy to the touch.

* As soon as the parkin comes out of the oven, cut into squares in the tin, cutting right down to the base and being careful not to scratch the tin. (This initial cutting is important because as the cake cools it becomes very firm and more difficult to cut.)

* Leave to cool in the tin for at least 30 minutes, then use the baking paper to lift the whole cake out of the tin and place on a wire rack to cool fully. Once cool, use a sharp knife to go over the initial cuts again, then separate the pieces.

* Store in an airtight container and eat within 7–10 days.

# FRUITY POWER FLAPJACKS

**Makes: 12 flapjacks**

Flapjacks are a brilliant snack to have in your cupboard in case of emergencies! They're portable and full of energy, so are great for taking in your bag to see you through a long day or night in the library. They also keep very well, so with a bit of restraint they can last you for up to a week.

Vegetable oil or butter, for greasing
250g butter
175g light brown soft sugar
150g golden syrup
300g porridge oats
100g dried cranberries
100g dried apricots, chopped
50g pecan halves

20cm square cake tin
Non-stick baking paper

**Tip:** Vary the fruit and nuts in these flapjacks according to your taste and budget. Sultanas, prunes and dates, walnuts, hazelnuts and desiccated coconut are all great to use.

* Preheat the oven to 150°C Fan/Gas Mark 3. Grease a 20cm square cake tin and line with non-stick baking paper.

* Melt the butter, sugar and syrup together in a saucepan over a low heat.

* Add the oats, fruit and nuts and stir well into the melted mixture, ensuring all the oats are covered in the liquid.

* Carefully transfer the mixture to the prepared tin. Spread out evenly and level the top.

* Bake the flapjack for 20–25 minutes until the edges have started to brown a little. Don't worry if there appears to be some excess butter on the top.

* As soon as the flapjack comes out of the oven, cut into slices in the tin, cutting right down to the base and being careful not to scratch the tin. (This initial cutting is important because as the flapjack cools it becomes very firm and more difficult to cut.)

* Leave to cool and firm up in the tin for an hour, then use the baking paper to lift the whole flapjack out of the tin and place on a wire rack to cool fully. Once cool, use a sharp knife to go over the initial cuts again, then separate the pieces.

* Store in an airtight container and eat within 7 days.

# ZESTY LEMON BARS

**Makes: 12–16 bars**

These lovely citrusy bars taste so fresh and summery. The butter shortbread base is topped with a tangy topping similar to lemon curd. They make a great dessert for summer parties or barbecues.

### For the base

Vegetable oil or butter, for greasing

250g butter, softened

150g caster sugar

1 tsp vanilla extract

250g plain flour

### For the lemon topping

4 medium eggs

350g caster sugar

120ml lemon juice (from approx. 4 lemons)

50g plain flour

Icing sugar, to dust

20cm square cake tin

Non-stick baking paper

For techniques in **bold** see pages 12–13.

* Grease a 20cm square cake tin well, line with non-stick baking paper and set aside.

* Start by making the base. In a large mixing bowl, **beat** together the butter and sugar until pale and fluffy.

* Add the vanilla extract and stir in, then **sift** in the flour and stir to form a smooth dough.

* Turn the mixture out into the cake tin and press down to cover the tin evenly. Cover with cling film and chill in the fridge for 30 minutes.

* Meanwhile, preheat the oven to 170°C Fan/Gas Mark 5.

* When the base has chilled, remove the cling film and bake for 15–20 minutes until it becomes firm, but not too brown.

* Allow the base to cool in the tin for 30 minutes once baked. Leave the oven turned on.

* Meanwhile, make the lemony topping. Place the eggs, sugar and lemon juice together in a bowl and **whisk** well.

* Sift the flour into the lemon mixture and whisk in.

* Pour the lemon topping mixture over the cooled base and bake at the same temperature as before for 25–30 minutes until the topping has firmed up – it should look browned and a little bubbly around the edges.

* Leave the bars to cool fully in the tin before attempting to cut them up, as they will be very liquid when warm. Once cool, it can be helpful to chill them even further in the fridge. Dust with icing sugar, then slice into bars, cutting carefully so as not to scratch the tin.

* Store in an airtight container and eat within 7 days.

# APPLE AND DATE LUMBERJACK SLICES

**Makes: 12 slices**

This is an old-fashioned recipe, so-called because it was supposedly eaten by American lumberjacks! Whether that's true or not, these unusual slices are likely to become a firm favourite, with their moist, fruity sponge and rich, buttery, coconut topping. Try them and see!

**For the base**

Vegetable oil or butter, for greasing

125g butter, softened

220g caster sugar

1 tsp vanilla extract

1 medium egg, beaten

145g dates, stoned and chopped

2 large apples, peeled, cored and chopped into 2cm chunks

1 tsp bicarbonate of soda

210g plain flour

230ml hot water

**For the topping**

60g butter

100g demerara sugar

50g desiccated coconut

2 tbsp milk

20cm square cake tin

Non-stick baking paper

For techniques in **bold** see pages 12–13.

* Preheat the oven to 180°C Fan/Gas Mark 6. Grease a 20cm square cake tin and line with non-stick baking paper.

* Start by making the base. In a large mixing bowl, **beat** together the butter and sugar until pale and fluffy.

* Add the vanilla extract and egg and mix in thoroughly, followed by the dates and apple – just stir these in gently.

* **Sift** in the bicarbonate of soda and flour and **fold** in gently, then add the hot water and stir. The batter will be very liquid.

* Pour the batter into the cake tin, bake for 45 minutes and remove from the oven. It will only be part-baked at this stage.

* Meanwhile, make the topping by placing the butter and sugar in a small saucepan and mixing well. Add the coconut and milk and stir together over a low heat until the butter is melted and the sugar is dissolved.

* Spoon the mixture, including any liquid, over the part-cooked base, just removed from the oven, and return the tin to the oven to bake for a further 15–20 minutes.

* Check if the cake is cooked by inserting a skewer or cocktail stick into the centre to see if it comes out clean. If it doesn't, return to the oven for a further 5 minutes and test again. Note that this cake is very moist, due to the apple chunks, and dries out further after an hour or two, so be careful not to overbake.

* Leave the cake to cool in the tin for at least 30 minutes before carefully transferring to a wire rack to cool fully. Cut into slices once cool.

* Store in an airtight container and eat within 7 days. Once cool, can be frozen in sealed freezer bags for up to 3 months.

# MARBLE CAKE SQUARES

**Makes: 16 squares**

These swirled squares are really easy to make and look very pretty. The combination of chocolate and vanilla sponge is simple, but really delicious.

Vegetable oil or butter,
for greasing
250g butter, softened
250g caster sugar
3 large eggs
250g self-raising flour
1 tsp baking powder
2 tsp vanilla extract
3 tbsp cocoa powder

20cm square cake tin
Non-stick baking paper

For techniques in **bold**
see pages 12–13.

* Preheat the oven to 170°C Fan/Gas Mark 5. Grease a 20cm square cake tin and line with non-stick baking paper.

* In a mixing bowl, **beat** together the butter and sugar until pale and fluffy.

* In a separate bowl, **whisk** the eggs. Add them to the butter and sugar mixture a little at a time, beating well after each addition until the cake batter is smooth and all the egg is mixed in.

* **Sift** in the flour and baking powder and **fold** in gently.

* Take a second mixing bowl and transfer half the cake batter into this bowl.

* Add the vanilla extract to one bowl of cake mixture and fold in gently.

* Sift the cocoa powder into the second bowl of cake mixture and fold in gently.

* Dollop alternate spoonfuls of cake batter into the prepared tin and use a knife or cocktail stick to swirl the mixtures together. Bake for 35–45 minutes until golden brown. Test the centre with a skewer or cocktail stick. It will come out clean if the cake is cooked. If not, return the cake to the oven for another 3 minutes and test again.

* Leave the cake to cool in the tin for 30 minutes, before removing from the tin and leaving to cool fully on a wire rack. Cut into squares once cool.

* Store in an airtight container and eat within 7 days. Once cool, the squares can be frozen in sealed freezer bags for up to 3 months.

# COCONUT CAKE BARS

**Makes: 12 large bars**

These are a coconut-lover's dream. The Malibu adds some tropical oomph to both the sponge and frosting and makes these something rather special. You can always use the rest of the bottle as an excuse to throw a party!

## For the cake base
Vegetable oil or butter,
for greasing

120g butter, softened

190g caster sugar

3 medium eggs, beaten

1 tbsp Malibu

Pinch of salt

180ml full-fat coconut milk

300g plain flour

1 tsp baking powder

50g desiccated coconut, plus

3 tbsp for sprinkling

## For the frosting
115g unsalted butter, softened

500g icing sugar, sifted

30ml coconut milk

2 tsp Malibu

20cm square cake tin

Non-stick baking paper

For techniques in **bold**
see pages 12–13.

* Preheat the oven to 170°C Fan/Gas Mark 5. Grease a 20cm square cake tin and line with non-stick baking paper.

* In a large mixing bowl, **beat** together the butter and sugar until pale and fluffy.

* Add the beaten eggs, a little at a time, and stir in well after each addition. Then add the Malibu, salt and coconut milk and stir in gently.

* **Sift** in the flour and baking powder and **fold** in gently, followed by the desiccated coconut.

* Pour the cake mixture into the prepared tin and bake for 35–45 minutes until browned and a skewer or cocktail stick inserted into the centre comes out clean. If it doesn't, return the cake to the oven for another 3 minutes and then test again.

* Leave the cake to cool in the tin for 30 minutes, before removing from the tin and leaving to cool fully on a wire rack.

* To make the frosting, in a large mixing bowl, mix the butter with roughly a third of the icing sugar until thoroughly combined and no longer dry. Gradually add another third of the sugar and mix until well combined. Finally, add the remaining icing sugar and mix in, then beat in the coconut milk and Malibu. Mix well until smooth and creamy.

* Ice the cake while whole, then sprinkle with 3 tablespoons of desiccated coconut, and cut into slices.

* Store in an airtight container in the fridge. Eat within 3 days.

# HUMMINGBIRD SLICES

**Makes: 12 slices**

This is a delicious, moist and fruity recipe that comes from the USA. It's a real crowd-pleaser too. In the unlikely event you have any of these left, they can be frozen, even with frosting, for up to three months.

Vegetable oil or butter, for greasing

170g self-raising flour

Pinch of salt

1 tsp baking powder

130g light brown soft sugar

40g desiccated coconut

250g mashed ripe bananas (approx. 2 large ones)

300g crushed pineapple in syrup, drained

3 large eggs, beaten

135ml sunflower oil

Cream Cheese Frosting (page 38)

20cm square cake tin

Non-stick baking paper

For techniques in **bold** see pages 12–13.

* Preheat the oven to 170°C Fan/Gas Mark 5. Grease a 20cm square cake tin and line with non-stick baking paper.

* **Sift** the flour, salt and baking powder into a large mixing bowl. Add the sugar and stir everything together well.

* Add the coconut, mashed banana, drained pineapple, beaten eggs and oil, and stir in to combine all ingredients evenly.

* Pour the mixture into the prepared cake tin and bake for 40–50 minutes until browned and a skewer or cocktail stick inserted into the centre comes out clean. If it doesn't, return the cake to the oven for another 3 minutes and then test again.

* Leave the cake to cool in the tin for 30 minutes, before removing from the tin and allowing to cool fully on a wire rack. Once completely cool, ice the cake with the Cream Cheese Frosting (page 38) and cut into slices .

* Store in an airtight container in the fridge. Eat within 3 days.

# BREAKFAST BAKING

# BANANA AND BLUEBERRY MUFFINS

**Makes: 12 muffins or 15 fairy cake-sized muffins**

Muffins make such a nice start to the day. These are light, fruity and easy to make – even with a hangover! You need never waste any brown bananas or soft blueberries again – this recipe is the perfect way to use up overripe fruit.

3 very ripe bananas

125ml sunflower oil

2 large eggs, beaten

100g caster sugar

150g plain flour

½ tsp bicarbonate of soda

1 tsp baking powder

150g blueberries

Muffin or fairy cake tray(s)

Paper cases

For techniques in **bold** see pages 12–13.

* Preheat the oven to 200°C Fan/Gas Mark 7. Line your muffin or fairy cake tray with the appropriately sized paper cases.

* In a medium bowl, mash the bananas well. Then add the oil, eggs and sugar, and mix to combine.

* **Sift** the flour, bicarbonate of soda and baking powder into a mixing bowl.

* Pour the banana mixture into the flour and mix very lightly until the flour is only just incorporated. Be careful not to overmix or the muffins can turn out dense and heavy.

* Add the blueberries and stir in very gently.

* Spoon the mixture into the cake cases and bake for 20–25 minutes for muffins or 18–22 minutes for fairy cakes until they are nicely golden brown on top.

* Allow to cool in the tin for 15 minutes before removing and placing on a wire rack to cool fully.

* Store in an airtight container and eat within 2–3 days. Once cool, can be frozen in sealed freezer bags for up to 3 months.

# BERRY AND OAT MUFFINS

**Makes: 12 muffins or 16 fairy cake-sized muffins**

*Lovely and fruity but not overly sweet, these muffins are packed with oats, which makes them substantial enough to stave off any mid-morning hunger pangs.*

325g plain flour

1½ tbsp baking powder

Pinch of bicarbonate of soda

Pinch of salt

200g light brown soft sugar

50g porridge oats

2 medium eggs

100ml milk

100g natural yoghurt

75ml sunflower oil

1 tsp vanilla extract

125g berries (blueberries, raspberries and blackberries work very well)

Muffin or fairy cake tray(s)

Paper cases

For techniques in **bold**
see pages 12–13.

* Preheat the oven to 180°C Fan/Gas Mark 6. Line your muffin or fairy cake tray with the appropriately sized paper cases.

* **Sift** the flour, baking powder, bicarbonate of soda and salt into a mixing bowl, add the sugar and oats, and stir together to combine well.

* Next, put the eggs, milk, yoghurt, oil and vanilla extract into a jug and **whisk** together well.

* Pour the wet ingredients into the dry ones and gently stir to combine. Try not to mix too much as this can cause the muffins to turn out dense and heavy.

* Add the berries and stir gently into the mixture.

* Spoon the muffin mixture into the cake cases and bake for 20–25 minutes for muffins and 15–20 minutes for fairy cakes until golden brown.

* Allow to cool in the tin for 15 minutes before removing and placing on a wire rack to cool fully.

* Store in an airtight container and eat within 2–3 days. Once cool, can be frozen in sealed freezer bags for up to 3 months.

# LEMON AND POPPY SEED MUFFINS

**Makes: 12 muffins or 16 fairy cake-sized muffins**

When it comes to muffin flavours, this is a real classic. The lemon zest balances out the sweetness of the sponge and the poppy seeds add a satisfying crunch.

225g plain flour

1 tsp bicarbonate of soda

165g light brown soft sugar

Pinch of salt

200ml milk

175ml sunflower
or vegetable oil

1 medium egg, beaten

Finely grated zest of 5 lemons

4 tbsp poppy seeds

Muffin or fairy cake tray(s)

Paper cases

For techniques in **bold**
see pages 12–13.

* Preheat the oven to 180°C Fan/Gas Mark 6. Line your muffin or fairy cake tray with the appropriately sized paper cases.

* **Sift** the flour and bicarbonate of soda into a mixing bowl. Add the sugar and salt and stir into the flour.

* Pour the milk, oil and beaten egg into the dry mixture and stir gently to form a sticky batter.

* Add the lemon zest and poppy seeds and stir until combined. Stop mixing as soon as the flour is incorporated and the seeds are evenly distributed, as overmixing can cause the muffins to turn out dense and heavy.

* Spoon the mixture evenly into the cake cases and bake for 25–30 minutes for muffins and 18–22 minutes for fairy cakes until golden brown and well risen.

* Allow to cool in the tin for 15 minutes before removing and placing on a wire rack to cool fully.

* Store in an airtight container and eat within 2–3 days. Once cool, can be frozen in sealed freezer bags for up to 3 months.

# CHEESE AND SPINACH MUFFINS

**Makes: 12 muffins or 15 fairy cake-sized muffins**

These savoury muffins are totally delicious and really easy to make. You can bake a batch in advance, as they freeze well. They are lovely on their own or with soup, and are perfect in a packed lunch.

350ml milk

2 tsp lemon juice

500g plain flour

2 tbsp baking powder

340g extra-mature Cheddar or Gruyère cheese, grated

100g cooked spinach, drained very well and chopped finely (see Tip)

Pinch of salt and plenty of black pepper

2 medium eggs

150ml sunflower or vegetable oil

Muffin or fairy cake tray(s)

Paper cases

For techniques in **bold** see pages 12–13.

* Preheat the oven to 180°C Fan/Gas Mark 6. Line your muffin or fairy cake tray with the appropriately sized paper cases.

* Pour the milk into a jug and add the lemon juice. Stir gently and set aside.

* **Sift** the flour and baking powder into a large mixing bowl, add the cheese, spinach and salt and pepper, and mix together well.

* Pour the eggs and oil into the milk and lemon and **whisk** together well.

* Pour the wet ingredients into the flour mixture and gently stir to form a thick batter. Be careful not to overmix as this can cause the muffins to turn out dense and heavy.

* Spoon the mixture into the cake cases (they will be pretty full) and bake for 25–30 minutes for muffins or 20–22 minutes for fairy cake-sized muffins, until golden brown. These savoury muffins don't tend to rise as much as sweet ones.

* Allow to cool in the tin for 15 minutes before removing and either eating warm or placing on a wire rack to cool fully.

* Store in an airtight container and eat within 2–3 days. Once cool, can be frozen in sealed freezer bags for up to 3 months.

**Tip:** Frozen spinach works better here than fresh. Once cooked, drain in a sieve, pressing down firmly with the back of a spoon to squeeze out as much water as possible before use.

# CHEDDAR SCONES

**Makes: approximately 8 scones**

Do not overlook the humble cheese scone. They are unbelievably simple to make and so tasty, especially when still warm from the oven. If you have any left after breakfast, they are great with soup for lunch.

225g self-raising flour, plus a little extra for the work surface
Pinch of salt
55g butter, cold and cubed
75g mature Cheddar, grated
150ml milk

Large baking sheet
Round cookie cutter (or glass)

For techniques in **bold**
see pages 12–13.

**Tip:** Ensure you use an extra-mature Cheddar when making these scones – it will make them much tastier.

* Preheat the oven to 220°C Fan/Gas Mark 9. Lightly grease a large baking sheet, line with non-stick baking paper and set aside.

* **Sift** the flour and salt into a large mixing bowl, add the butter and rub into the flour using your fingertips until the mixture looks like breadcrumbs.

* Stir in 25g of the cheese and add the milk. Bring the mixture together to form a very soft dough.

* Ensure your work surface is clean and lightly dust with flour. Tip the scone dough out onto the floured area and **knead** very gently to bring the dough together into a soft ball.

* Roll the dough out to about 2cm thick and stamp out rounds using a 4–6cm cookie cutter or a clean drinking glass. Place the rounds onto the prepared baking sheet.

* Lightly knead together the rest of the dough and roll out again, then cut out more scones and repeat until all the dough has been used.

* Top the scones with the remaining cheese. Bake for around 12–15 minutes until well risen and golden.

* Allow to cool on the sheet for 10 minutes before transferring to a wire rack to cool fully.

* Store in an airtight container and eat within 2–3 days. Once cool, can be frozen in sealed freezer bags for up to 3 months.

# CINNAMON BUNS

**Makes: 9 buns**

You can't beat a freshly baked cinnamon bun for breakfast, or at any time of the day for that matter. They're just so good. Although they take a little bit of time to make, you'll realise they're worth the effort when you take your first bite. Try adding sultanas or chopped nuts to the filling for something different.

## For the dough

215g plain flour, plus a little extra for the work surface

215g strong white bread flour

Pinch of salt

75g caster sugar

2 tsp quick-action dried yeast

230ml milk

75g butter

1 large egg, beaten

Vegetable oil, for greasing

## For the filling

85g butter, softened

75g demerara sugar

4 tsp ground cinnamon

50g raisins and/or chopped nuts (optional)

## For the topping

1 large egg, beaten

3 tbsp demerara sugar

20cm square cake tin

Non-stick baking paper

For techniques in **bold** see pages 12–13.

* Start by making the dough. **Sift** both types of flour into a large mixing bowl. Add the salt, sugar and yeast, and stir well.

* Place the milk and butter into a saucepan over a low heat and allow the butter to melt. Do not let the milk simmer.

* Pour the milk and melted butter into the flour mixture and stir to form a stiff dough.

* Add the egg and continue to stir together to form a soft dough.

* Grease a large mixing bowl with oil and place the dough into the bowl. Cover with lightly oiled cling film and place in a warm place for around 45 minutes until the dough has risen.

* Meanwhile, make the filling by **beating** together the butter, sugar and cinnamon, and add the raisins and chopped nuts if you are using them.

* Grease a 20cm square cake tin and line with non-stick baking paper and set aside. When the dough has risen, remove from the bowl and place on a clean, floured work surface. Gently roll out the dough to form a rectangle around 2cm thick, no thinner.

* Spread the filling evenly over the dough. If the butter has become firm, you can break it up into pieces and distribute evenly over the dough.

* Now, roll up the dough to form the buns by placing your dough in a landscape position in front of you and, starting from one of the long sides of the rectangle, rolling up the dough like a Swiss roll.

* Cut the roll of dough into nine slices. Each slice should be about 4–5cm thick. Fit the buns into your prepared tin, cover

with cling film and allow them to rise for a further 30 minutes in a warm place.

* Meanwhile, preheat the oven to 180°C Fan/Gas Mark 6 .

* When the buns have risen, brush them with the beaten egg, sprinkle over the demerara sugar and bake for 25–35 minutes until golden brown.

* Remove the buns from the tray, without separating them, and leave to cool on a wire rack for 20 minutes before pulling apart and diving in. These are best eaten while still warm, and within 24 hours.

* Store in an airtight container and eat within 1–2 days.

# BREAKFAST FRUIT LOAF

**Serves: 8–10**

This gorgeous spicy fruit bread is perfect for brekkie. Simply slice and butter when freshly baked. After a day or two it's better toasted.

Vegetable oil or butter,
for greasing

465g strong white bread flour,
plus extra for the work surface

2 tsp ground cinnamon

65g caster sugar,
plus 2 tsp for sprinkling

2 tsp quick-action dried yeast

365ml warm water
(around body temperature)

2 tsp milk

200g sultanas

900g loaf tin
Non-stick baking paper

For techniques in **bold**
see pages 12–13.

* Grease a 900g loaf tin and line with non-stick baking paper.

* **Sift** the flour and cinnamon into a mixing bowl and add the sugar and yeast.

* Add the warm water, milk and sultanas. Make sure the water is roughly body temperature – warm enough to activate the yeast, but not too hot or it can kill the yeast. Mix well for a couple of minutes to bring the mixture together into a soft, sticky dough. Turn it out onto a clean, well-floured work surface.

* **Knead** the dough for 8–10 minutes. It will become much smoother and less sticky by the time you have finished.

* Lightly coat the inside of a large mixing bowl with oil. Place the dough into the bowl and cover with a lightly oiled piece of cling film. Leave the dough in a warm place for an hour or so until it has doubled in size.

* Take the dough out of the mixing bowl, place on a well-floured work surface again, and knead for 5 minutes.

* Place the dough into the prepared tin, cover with oiled cling film and leave to rise for another 30 minutes. Meanwhile, preheat the oven to 200°C Fan/Gas Mark 7.

* When the dough has risen for the second time, remove the cling film and sprinkle with the remaining 2 teaspoons of sugar.

* Bake for 40–50 minutes until well risen and browned. Remove the loaf from the tin and tap the bottom to test if it's cooked. It will sound hollow if cooked. If not, place back in the tin and return to the oven for a further 5 minutes, then test again.

* Remove the loaf from the tin and allow to cool on a wire rack before slicing.

* Store in an airtight container and eat within 2–3 days. Once cool, the loaf or slices can be frozen in a sealed freezer bag for up to 3 months.

# AMERICAN PANCAKES

**Makes: 6 pancakes (7–10cm)**

Who doesn't love pancakes in the morning? These are thicker than English pancakes, and the good news is that they are quick and easy to make. Stir a few blueberries into the batter before cooking and serve scattered with orange zest, or try them topped with sliced banana and maple syrup.

135g plain flour

½ tsp salt

1 tbsp caster sugar

1 tsp baking powder

145ml milk

1 medium egg

Butter, for cooking

A large handful of blueberries (optional)

Maple syrup, to dress

Finely grated orange zest, to decorate

For techniques in **bold** see pages 12–13.

* In a bowl, combine the plain flour, salt, sugar and baking powder, and stir together evenly.

* Place the milk into a jug. Crack in the egg and **whisk** together using a fork. When well mixed, pour this mixture into the bowl containing the dry ingredients.

* Stir the mixture together gently until all the flour is mixed in. Don't worry about any lumps.

* Set the mixture aside for 10 minutes. If you wish, stir in the blueberries just before using the mixture.

* Melt a knob of butter in a large frying pan over a low heat and swirl it around so that the base of the pan is evenly covered in butter. Now, turn the heat up so that the pan starts to become quite hot.

* When the butter is bubbling, pour in two separate dollops of mixture (roughly 2 heaped tablespoons per pancake). Leave the pancakes to cook without touching them for a minute or two until you notice several holes developing on the surface. Now you are ready to flip the pancakes.

* Cook for another couple of minutes on the other side until they are brown on both sides.

* Keep warm within silver foil, while you cook the remaining pancakes in the same way.

* Stack the pancakes in a pile on a serving plate and drizzle with maple syrup. Decorate with orange zest, or serve with your topping of choice.

# BUDGET GRANOLA

**Makes: 15 servings**

Granola is a mixture of oats and seeds, a bit like muesli. It can be really pricey to buy, and many recipes call for expensive ingredients. So here is a much cheaper version to make at home. It's delicious with milk, or sprinkled on yoghurt and fruit for breakfast, or even eaten on its own as a wholesome snack during the day. Try it on ice cream!

200g porridge oats

70g sunflower seeds

50g desiccated coconut

1 tsp ground cinnamon

2 tsp vanilla extract

150g runny honey

4 tsp fruit juice

100g dried cranberries, sultanas or apricots (or a mixture)

Large baking sheet

Non-stick baking paper

* Preheat the oven to 160°C Fan/Gas Mark 4. Line a large baking sheet with non-stick baking paper and set aside.

* Measure out the oats, seeds, coconut and cinnamon and place in a bowl.

* Add the vanilla extract, honey and fruit juice and stir into the dry ingredients well.

* Tip the granola out onto the prepared baking sheet and spread out evenly.

* Bake for 20 minutes, then remove from the oven and stir well. Return to the oven and bake for a further 15–20 minutes until the granola is an even golden brown.

* Allow to cool fully, then stir through the dried fruit. Store in an airtight container for up to 2 months.

# APRICOT WHIRLS

**Makes: 12 small pastries**

A quick and easy breakfast pastry, these whirls look a bit like apricot sausage rolls! They use only store-cupboard ingredients, making them very convenient to rustle up whenever you fancy something yummy for breakfast.

375g pack of ready-made, ready-rolled puff pastry, fridge-cold

450g apricot jam

12 apricot halves, fresh or from a tin and drained

1 medium egg, beaten

1 tbsp icing sugar, for dusting

Large baking sheet
Non-stick baking paper

* Preheat the oven to 200°C Fan/Gas Mark 7. Line a baking sheet with non-stick baking paper and set aside.

* Unroll the pastry and cut the sheet in half lengthways to give you two wide rectangles.

* Spread half the jam evenly over each piece of pastry, leaving a 2cm margin around the edges.

* Make sure the pastry is sat in front of you in a landscape position, then lay out six apricot halves next to each other lengthways along the bottom of each pastry sheet.

* Brush the edges of the pastry with beaten egg and fold the length of pastry over the top of the apricots. Flip it over, so that the apricots can't fall out, and then roll up entirely. Repeat with the other roll.

* Slice each roll into six, cutting in between the apricots, and carefully place each whirl on the prepared baking sheet.

* Brush the whirls well with the beaten egg and bake for 20–25 minutes until the pastry is golden brown and crispy.

* Allow to cool on the sheet for 10 minutes, then serve while warm, dusted with icing sugar if you like. Any remaining whirls should be stored in an airtight container and are best eaten within 24 hours.

# HOT CHEESE AND TOMATO PASTRIES

**Makes: 8 pastries**

When you fancy something savoury and full of flavour in the morning, these really hit the spot. They look impressive, but are actually very easy to put together.

375g pack of ready-made, ready-rolled puff pastry, fridge-cold

8 x 1 tsp tomato chutney

8 cherry tomatoes, halved

125g ball of mozzarella, torn into small pieces

1 large egg, beaten

Large baking sheet
Non-stick baking paper

* Preheat the oven to 200°C Fan/Gas Mark 7. Line a baking sheet with non-stick baking paper and set aside.

* Unwrap the pastry and cut it into eight evenly sized rectangles.

* Place a teaspoon of tomato chutney in the centre of each square. Using the back of the spoon, spread it out a little over the pastry.

* Now place two cherry tomato halves on each pastry, on top of the tomato chutney.

* Divide the mozzarella cheese evenly among the pastries and place on top of the tomatoes and chutney.

* Gently pull up each corner of the pastry towards the centre so that they just meet in the middle.

* Transfer the pastries to the prepared baking sheet and brush well with beaten egg.

* Bake for 20–25 minutes until the pastry is golden brown and the filling is bubbling. Serve while still hot.

* Store in an airtight container and eat within 1–2 days.

# EASY BREADS

# CRUSTY WHITE LOAF

**Makes: 1 large loaf**

If you've ever wondered why you might want to make your own bread when it's so much quicker to buy it, give this recipe a go, and you'll soon understand. It's great fun to make – and delicious!

500g strong white bread flour, plus extra for dusting the work surface

1 tsp salt

1 tsp caster sugar

1 tbsp quick-action dried yeast

300ml warm water (around body temperature)

Vegetable or sunflower oil, for greasing

900g loaf tin

Non-stick baking paper

For techniques in **bold** see pages 12–13.

**Tips:** If you are struggling to find a warm place for your dough to rise, you can try a sunny windowsill. Or you can cover the dough with a tea towel (over the cling film) and leave next to the switched-on oven.

* **Sift** the flour and salt into a large mixing bowl, then stir in the sugar and yeast.

* Pour the water into the flour mixture and mix well to bring the dough together into a sticky ball.

* Cover the bowl with cling film and set it aside in a warm place for an hour, until the mixture has doubled in size (known as 'rising').

* Grease a 900g loaf tin well and line with non-stick baking paper.

* When the dough has risen well, turn it out onto a clean, floured work surface and **knead** for 5–10 minutes until smooth and elastic. It will decrease in size again, but that's fine.

* Form the dough into a ball, place it seam-side down into the loaf tin, cover with cling film and leave in a warm spot for 30 minutes to rise again.

* Meanwhile, preheat the oven to 200°C Fan/Gas Mark 7.

* Once the dough has risen in the tin, remove the cling film and bake the loaf for 30–40 minutes until golden and crusty.

* To check whether the loaf is cooked, turn it out of the tin and tap it on the bottom. If it is, it will sound hollow. If not, place it back in the tin and return to the oven for a further 5 minutes, then test again. Enjoy while warm.

* Store in an airtight container and eat within 2–3 days. Once cool, can be frozen in a sealed freezer bag for up to 3 months. If you want to toast it from frozen, remember to slice it first.

# CHEESE AND ONION BREAD

**Makes: 1 large loaf**

This is a delicious loaf, packed with mature Cheddar cheese and onions. It is quite strongly flavoured, so it's great simply buttered or dipped in soup, but it makes very good sandwiches, too.

Knob of butter, for frying

½ small white onion, peeled and chopped into 1cm pieces

500g strong white bread flour

1 tsp salt

1 tsp caster sugar

1 tsp quick-action dried yeast

250ml warm water (around body temperature)

75ml milk

Vegetable or sunflower oil, for greasing

150g mature Cheddar cheese, grated

900g loaf tin

For techniques in **bold** see pages 12–13.

* Melt the butter in a frying pan, add the onion and allow to cook gently over a low heat for 15 minutes or so. You want the onion to soften until it is translucent – don't let it brown. Set aside.

* **Sift** the flour and salt into a large mixing bowl, add the sugar and yeast and mix well. Make a well in the middle of the bowl.

* Pour the warm water and milk into the well in the flour mixture. Make sure the water is roughly body temperature – warm enough to activate the yeast, but not too hot or it can kill the yeast and the bread won't rise. Mix in the liquids, to form a stiff dough.

* Cover the bowl with cling film and leave it in a warm place for an hour or so, until the dough has doubled in size (or 'risen').

* Grease a 900g loaf tin with oil, then dust it with flour.

* When the dough has risen well, turn it out onto a clean, well-floured work surface and **knead** for 5–8 minutes until smooth and ever so slightly sticky. It will decrease in size again.

* Stretch the dough out into a large rectangle. Scatter the onion and two-thirds of the cheese over the dough and roll it up from one of the long sides, like a Swiss roll, so that it will fit in the loaf tin.

* Place the dough into the tin, cover with cling film and leave in a warm place for 30 minutes to rise again. Meanwhile, preheat the oven to 220°C Fan/Gas Mark 9.

* Once the dough has risen, sprinkle the top with the remaining cheese and bake for 30–35 minutes until golden and well risen. To check the loaf is cooked, turn out of the tin and tap the base. If cooked, it will sound hollow. If not, place back in the tin and return to the oven for a further 5 minutes, then test again.

* Store in an airtight container and eat within 2–3 days. Once cool, can be frozen in a sealed freezer bag for up to 3 months. If you want to toast it from frozen, remember to slice it first.

# QUICK AND EASY CORNBREAD

**Serves: 4–6 generously**

Cornbread is very popular in America and is delicious served with stews, casseroles or chilli con carne. It's best eaten very fresh and doesn't keep for long, so it's great to make to share with friends. It's also one of the easiest breads you can make! Try adding 1 teaspoon of dried chilli flakes to the batter for an extra kick.

Vegetable or sunflower oil, for greasing

65g self-raising flour

2 tsp baking powder

1 tsp salt

220g fine-ground polenta or fine cornmeal

2 tsp caster sugar

75g butter, melted

275ml milk

50ml plain full-fat yoghurt

2 large eggs, beaten

1 tsp dried chilli flakes (optional)

20cm square cake tin

Non-stick baking paper

For techniques in **bold** see pages 12–13.

* Preheat the oven to 200°C Fan/Gas Mark 7. Grease a 20cm square baking tin, line with non-stick baking paper and set aside.

* **Sift** the flour, baking powder and salt into a large bowl, add the polenta or cornmeal and the sugar, and stir together well.

* Pour in the melted butter, milk and yoghurt, and stir in well.

* Finally, add the beaten eggs and stir to combine.

* Pour the batter into the prepared tin and bake for 18–22 minutes until it is lightly golden and springy to the touch.

* Leave to cool in the tin for 20 minutes to firm up, and then remove, cut into slices and enjoy while still warm.

* Once cool, the cornbread can be frozen in a sealed freezer bag for up to 3 months.

# WHOLEMEAL SODA BREAD

**Makes: 1 loaf**

This is possibly the easiest loaf of bread you will ever make. It's called soda bread because it uses bicarbonate of soda instead of yeast to get it to rise, which is a pretty foolproof method. It has a lovely flavour and is ideal for breakfast, sandwiches or to serve with a meal. It doesn't stay fresh for long but luckily freezes very well, which is great if you can't manage a whole loaf in a few days.

Vegetable or sunflower oil, for greasing

400ml milk

1 tbsp lemon juice

300g wholemeal flour

300g plain flour, plus extra for the work surface

1 tsp salt

1 tsp bicarbonate of soda

2 tbsp melted butter

Large baking sheet
Non-stick baking paper

For techniques in **bold** see pages 12–13.

* Preheat the oven to 230°C Fan/Gas Mark 9. Grease a large baking sheet, line with non-stick baking paper and set aside.

* Combine the milk and lemon juice and stir gently. Set aside.

* **Sift** both types of flour into a large mixing bowl, add the salt and bicarbonate of soda and mix. Make a well in the centre of the mixture.

* Pour the milk mixture and the melted butter into the well in the flour, and mix until all the flour is combined. You will have a wet and slightly sticky dough.

* Generously flour your work surface (make sure it is clean and dry first!) and turn the dough out onto the floured surface. **Knead** gently for 2–3 minutes, then shape into a ball.

* Using the handle of a wooden spoon, press a cross into the top of the loaf.

* Transfer the dough to the baking sheet and bake for around 40–45 minutes until golden brown on top.

* To check whether the loaf is cooked, turn it out of the tin and tap it on the bottom. If it is, it will sound hollow. If not, place it back in the tin and return to the oven for a further 5 minutes, then test again.

* Allow the loaf to cool on a wire rack for at least 30 minutes before slicing.

* Store in an airtight container and eat within 1–2 days. Once cool, can be frozen in a sealed freezer bag for up to 3 months. If you want to toast it from frozen, remember to slice it first.

# SULTANA SODA BREAD

**Makes: 1 loaf**

This is another easy soda bread, perfect for busy students as it's so simple to make – and delicious buttered or toasted. It is slightly sweet, so it's more of a breakfast or teatime loaf than one for sandwiches. It does go stale quite quickly, so if you can't eat it up in a day or two, just slice it and pop it in the freezer. Then, you're minutes away from hot, buttered toast whenever you fancy – you can toast it from frozen!

Vegetable or sunflower oil, for greasing

400ml milk

1 tbsp lemon juice

500g plain flour

1 tsp salt

1 tsp bicarbonate of soda

75g caster sugar

25g butter, melted

75g sultanas

900g loaf tin
Non-stick baking paper

For techniques in **bold** see pages 12–13.

* Preheat the oven to 200°C Fan/Gas Mark 7. Grease a 900g loaf tin, line with non-stick baking paper and set aside.

* Measure out the milk, add the lemon juice and stir gently. Set aside.

* **Sift** the flour into a large mixing bowl, add the salt, bicarbonate of soda and sugar and mix. Make a well in the centre of the mixture.

* Pour the milk mixture and melted butter into the well in the flour, and mix until all the flour is combined. You will have a wet and slightly sticky dough.

* Add the sultanas and stir to combine evenly.

* Pour the bread mixture into the loaf tin and bake for around 30–35 minutes until golden brown on top. To check whether the loaf is cooked, turn it out of the tin and tap it on the bottom. If it is, it will sound hollow. If not, place it back in the tin and return to the oven for a further 5 minutes, then test again.

* Once cooked, remove the loaf from the tin and allow to cool on a wire rack for at least 30 minutes before slicing.

* Store in an airtight container and eat within 1–2 days. Once cool, can be frozen in a sealed freezer bag for up to 3 months. If you want to toast it from frozen, remember to slice it first.

# CARAWAY SODA BREAD

**Makes: 1 loaf**

This easy soda bread is a great recipe for any beginner breadmaker who wants to try something unusual but still very simple. Flavoured with caraway, which has a lovely aniseed flavour, it makes an interesting change from normal bread. The finished loaf is delicious buttered, or toasted and topped with scrambled eggs.

Vegetable or sunflower oil,
for greasing

400ml milk

1 tbsp lemon juice

450g plain flour

2 tsp bicarbonate of soda

1 tsp salt

1 tsp caster sugar

2 tsp caraway seeds

900g loaf tin

Non-stick baking paper

For techniques in **bold**
see pages 12–13.

* Preheat the oven to 220°C Fan/Gas Mark 9. Grease a 900g loaf tin, line with non-stick baking paper and set aside.

* Place the milk in a jug and add the lemon juice. Stir gently and set aside.

* **Sift** the flour, bicarbonate of soda and salt into a large bowl. Add the sugar and caraway seeds and stir well to combine.

* Pour the milk and lemon juice mixture in and stir to bring the mixture together to a wet, sticky dough.

* Pour the mixture into the prepared tin and bake for 25–30 minutes until golden brown on top. To check whether the loaf is cooked, turn it out of the tin and tap it on the bottom. If it is, it will sound hollow. If not, place it back in the tin and return to the oven for a further 5 minutes, then test again.

* Leave the loaf to cool in the tin for 10 minutes or so before turning out and placing on a wire rack. Then leave to cool for another 20 minutes or so before slicing.

* Store in an airtight container and eat within 1–2 days. Once cool, can be frozen in a sealed freezer bag for up to 3 months. If you want to toast it from frozen, remember to slice it first.

# CARAMELISED ONION ROLLS

**Makes: 6–8 rolls**

These rolls taste so good filled with cheese for a packed lunch. They're amazing with soups or great with casseroles to mop up the juices.

2 large white onions, peeled and chopped thinly into half-moon shapes

1 tbsp vegetable or sunflower oil, plus extra for greasing

15g butter

1 tsp caster sugar

500g strong white bread flour, plus extra for dusting the work surface

2 tsp quick-action dried yeast

300ml warm water (around body temperature)

Salt and pepper

Large baking sheet
Non-stick baking paper

For techniques in **bold** see pages 12–13.

**Tip:** These rolls are best eaten fresh, so if you have any left over, freeze them individually. You can get them out of the freezer the night before you need them and they will be defrosted by the morning, ready for your choice of filling.

* Place the onion, oil and butter into a large frying pan. Cook gently over a medium heat to allow the onion to soften and become translucent. This will take about 15–20 minutes. Keep an eye on the temperature – you do not want it too hot or the onions will burn.

* Now, sprinkle the sugar over the onion, followed by some salt and pepper. Stir well and set the onion aside to cool.

* While the onion is cooling, make the dough. **Sift** the flour and 1 teaspoon of salt into a large mixing bowl. Add the yeast and stir well. Pour in the warm water and stir in. Make sure the water is roughly body temperature – warm enough to activate the yeast, but not too hot or it can kill the yeast and the bread won't rise. Bring the mixture together to form a sticky dough.

* Make sure your work surface is clean, and sprinkle some flour onto it. Tip the dough out onto the floured surface; it will be really sticky, so flour your hands too (and keep flouring them whenever you need to).

* Stretch the dough out into a large rectangle and place the cooled onion into the middle. Fold the edges into the centre, over the onions, and start to **knead**. This will be a bit awkward at first, and the onion will spill out, but keep kneading and after around 8–10 minutes you will have a smooth dough with the onion well incorporated.

* Lightly coat the inside of a large mixing bowl with oil. Place the dough into the bowl, cover with cling film, and leave in a warm place for an hour or so. It should double in size (or 'rise'). Meanwhile, grease a large baking sheet, line with non-stick baking paper and set aside.

* When the dough has risen well, flour a clean work surface

again, tip the dough out and knead gently just for a minute or two to knock out the air.

* Pinch off pieces of dough and gently form into balls (for large rolls, around the size of a tennis ball, or slightly smaller for medium-sized rolls). Place on the prepared baking sheet, ensuring they are well spaced as they will expand.

* Sprinkle the rolls with a little flour and cover loosely with cling film. Leave in a warm place for 20 minutes to rise again. Meanwhile, preheat the oven to 200°C Fan/Gas Mark 7.

* Once the rolls have risen, remove the cling film and bake in the preheated oven. Large rolls need 30–35 minutes, and medium rolls need 25–30 minutes.

* To check whether the rolls are cooked, tap them on the bottom. It they are, they will sound hollow. If not, return them to the oven for a further 5 minutes, then test again.

* Leave to cool on a wire rack for at least 20 minutes.

* Store in an airtight container and eat within 2–3 days. Once cool, can be frozen in sealed freezer bags for up to 3 months.

# CHEESY COURGETTE CATERPILLAR BREAD

**Makes: 1 large loaf**

This loaf is made up of cheesy rolls baked in a line to look like a caterpillar. Courgette might seem a strange ingredient but it makes the bread light and moist – just remember to squeeze excess water out of the grated courgettes so that the dough isn't too soggy.

500g strong white bread flour, plus extra for dusting the work surface

1 tsp salt

1 tsp quick-action dried yeast

2 tsp caster sugar

250ml warm water (around body temperature)

1 large courgette, grated and excess water squeezed out

100g mature Cheddar cheese, grated

Vegetable or sunflower oil, for greasing

Large baking sheet
Non-stick baking paper

For techniques in **bold** see pages 12–13.

**Tip:** This dough is quite wet and may feel very sticky. Just add a little extra flour if it helps you knead and shape it.

* **Sift** the flour and salt into a large mixing bowl, add the yeast and sugar and stir together.

* Pour in the warm water. Make sure the water is roughly body temperature – warm enough to activate the yeast, but not too hot or it can kill the yeast and the bread won't rise. Mix well to form a sticky dough.

* Turn out the dough onto a clean, floured work surface and **knead** for 8 minutes, then add the courgette and cheese and continue to knead until they are worked in. The dough will be wet at first, but will become smooth and only slightly sticky.

* Lightly oil the inside of a large mixing bowl. Place the dough in the bowl, cover with cling film and leave in a warm place for an hour or so, until the dough doubles in size (or 'rises'). Meanwhile, grease a large baking sheet and line with non-stick baking paper.

* Once the dough has risen, turn out onto a clean, floured work surface and knead again gently for a couple of minutes. Divide the mixture into six pieces and roll into balls. Place them touching each other in a line on the prepared baking sheet.

* Cover with cling film and leave in a warm place for 30 minutes to rise again. Meanwhile, preheat the oven to 200°C Fan/Gas Mark 7.

* When the dough has risen, sprinkle with flour, then bake for 30–40 minutes until golden brown and crusty. To test if the loaf is cooked, tap on the bottom. If ready, it will sound hollow. If not, return to the oven for a further 5 minutes, then test again. Leave to cool on a wire rack.

* Store in an airtight container and eat within 2–3 days. Once cool, can be frozen in a sealed freezer bag for up to 3 months.

# ARTISAN LOAF

**Makes: 1 loaf**

This loaf of bread might look and sound posh but it's an absolute doddle to make and will fool your friends into thinking you've bought it from an expensive bakery! It's excellent for everyday use, especially for serving with meals. Its delicious crust makes it ideal for mopping up stews or juices on your plate.

**400g strong white bread flour, plus extra for dusting**

**1 tsp salt**

**1 tsp quick-action dried yeast**

**1 tsp caster sugar**

**275ml warm water (around body temperature)**

**Vegetable or sunflower oil, for greasing**

**Large baking sheet**

For techniques in **bold** see pages 12–13.

**Tip:** Don't be tempted to skip the steam bath here – it's what makes this loaf so good.

* **Sift** the flour and salt into a large bowl, add the yeast and sugar and mix well to combine all the ingredients evenly.

* Add the warm water. Make sure the water is roughly body temperature – warm enough to activate the yeast, but not too hot as it can kill the yeast and the bread won't rise. Mix well, bringing together to form a sticky dough. Turn out onto a floured work surface and **knead** for 5 minutes.

* Lightly oil the inside of a large mixing bowl. Place the dough in the bowl and cover well with cling film. Leave in a warm spot for an hour or so until it has doubled in size (or 'risen').

* When the dough has risen well, turn it out of the bowl onto a floured work surface and knead again for 5–10 minutes until smooth and elastic.

* Grease a baking sheet with oil, then dust with flour. Place the dough onto the tray. Shape into an oval.

* Take a large sheet of cling film and completely cover one side with sunflower oil. Cover the loaf with the cling film (oiled-side down, in contact with the dough) and leave to rise again in a warm place for another hour. Make sure the cling film is not pulled too tight over the bread, as it will expand during this time. The oil stops the cling film from sticking to the dough.

* Meanwhile, position two shelves in your oven, one in the middle and the other at the bottom. Find your largest roasting tin and place it on the bottom shelf. Now preheat the oven to 200°C Fan/Gas Mark 7.

* Once the dough has risen again, put the kettle on to boil. Remove the cling film from the dough and sprinkle with a little

more flour. Use a sharp knife to cut three or four diagonal slashes across the top of the loaf.

* Place the baking sheet with the loaf on the top oven shelf. Wearing oven gloves, carefully pull out the bottom shelf just a little so that you can safely pour water from the boiled kettle into the roasting tin. Half-fill the tin with the boiling water. This will create steam in the oven, which helps your bread to develop a nice crust.

* Bake the bread for around 40 minutes until risen, golden brown and crusty. To test whether the loaf is cooked, turn it out of the tin and tap it on the bottom. If it is, it will sound hollow. If not, return to the oven for a further 5 minutes, then test again.

* Allow the loaf to cool for 10 minutes on a wire rack, then slice and enjoy while still warm.

* Store in an airtight container and eat within 2–3 days. Once cool, can be frozen in sealed freezer bags for up to 3 months. If you want to toast it from frozen, remember to slice it first.

# HOMEMADE PIZZA BASE

**Serves: 1–2 (makes 1 large pizza base)**

You can't beat a homemade pizza. They are much tastier and cheaper than takeaway pizzas or frozen ones from the supermarket. Once you've mastered the base, you can jazz it up with various toppings. If you're cooking for a crowd, simply multiply the recipe accordingly to make more bases, and have plenty of toppings to hand.

**200g strong white bread flour,
plus extra for dusting
and shaping**

**½ tsp salt**

**⅓ tsp quick-action dried yeast**

**¼ tsp caster sugar**

**125ml warm water
(around body temperature)**

**2 tsp olive oil**

**Various toppings (see Tip)**

**Large baking sheet**

For techniques in **bold**
see pages 12–13.

**Tip:** To turn your pizza base into a delicious dinner, just add your favourite toppings. The pizza shown here is topped with tomato sauce, spinach, mozarella and black olives, with an egg cooked in the middle (see photos overleaf).

* **Sift** the flour and salt into a large mixing bowl, add the yeast and sugar and mix to combine.

* Add the warm water and 1 teaspoon of the olive oil. Make sure the water is roughly body temperature – warm enough to activate the yeast, but not too hot as it can kill the yeast. Mix well until the ingredients come together to form a sticky dough.

* Turn the dough out onto a floured work surface and **knead** gently for a couple of minutes until the dough feels smoother.

* Place the dough into a bowl, cover with cling film and a clean tea towel and leave in a warm place for an hour to rise. This can be near a warm oven or in the sunlight near the window. The dough should almost double in size.

* If you are going to eat your pizza immediately, preheat the oven to 220°C Fan/Gas Mark 9 and grease a large baking sheet with the remaining teaspoon of olive oil.

* Turn out the dough onto a lightly floured surface again and knead gently for around 5 minutes until it feels smooth, less sticky and elastic.

* Roll out the dough and, with floury hands, shape into a round as thick or thin as you prefer. If you wish to freeze the dough, now is the time (wrap the base in cling film and freeze for up to 3 months; then defrost completely before adding toppings and baking). Otherwise, transfer the dough to the baking sheet and add your toppings.

* Bake for 10 minutes, then slide the pizza off the baking sheet directly onto the oven shelf and bake for another 2–3 minutes until the base is golden and crispy and the toppings are cooked.

* Serve straight away. Any leftovers are great cold for a packed lunch the next day.

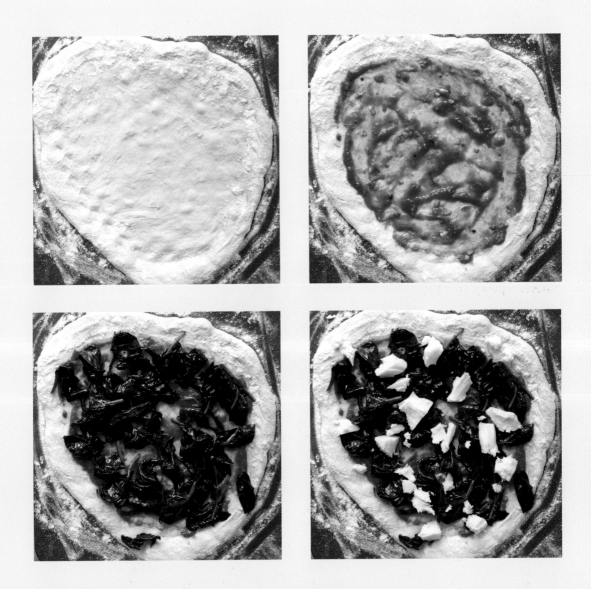

# HOMEMADE TORTILLAS

**Makes: 4 small tortillas**

These tortillas are a great homemade version of shop-bought wraps.
They're really satisfying to eat when still warm, as a sandwich, or to
dip into houmous, guacamole or chilli con carne. They don't require
much in the way of ingredients, so this is an ideal recipe to turn to
when your cupboard is really bare.

120g self-raising flour,
plus extra for dusting the
work surface

Pinch of salt

1½ tsp vegetable
or sunflower oil

4 tbsp warm water

For techniques in **bold**
see pages 12–13.

* **Sift** the flour and salt into a large bowl, then add the oil and water. Mix well to form a stiff dough.

* Divide the mixture into four balls. Place one ball at a time onto a clean, floured work surface. Roll each out into a thin circle.

* Place a large non-stick frying pan over a high heat. When the pan is really hot, place one of the dough circles into the dry pan and cook for 30–50 seconds on each side. Flip the tortilla when it is just lightly brown.

* Lift the cooked tortilla out of the pan with a spatula or fish slice and immediately wrap in foil to keep warm while you cook the rest. Repeat with the rest of the dough circles until all the tortillas are cooked.

* Once cool, the tortillas can be frozen in sealed freezer bags for up to 3 months.

# FLATBREADS

**Makes: 4 flatbreads**

Flatbreads are extremely versatile — great to mop up curries and stews, or to tear up and enjoy with dips. They can also be used to bulk out a meal if you're cooking for friends.

275g strong white bread flour, plus extra for the work surface

Pinch of salt

1 tsp quick-action dried yeast

1 tbsp olive oil

180ml warm water (around body temperature)

For techniques in **bold** see pages 12–13.

* **Sift** the flour and salt into a bowl, add the yeast and mix well.

* Add the oil and warm water. Make sure the water is roughly body temperature – warm enough to activate the yeast, but not too hot to kill it. Mix well to form a soft and sticky dough.

* Turn out onto a floured work surface and **knead** for 5 minutes. Lightly coat the inside of a large mixing bowl with oil. Place the dough in the bowl, cover with cling film and leave in a warm place for 20 minutes to rise.

* After the dough has risen, divide it into four pieces and place one piece at a time on a clean and well-floured work surface. Knead lightly and roll each piece out into a large circle.

* Place a large non-stick frying pan over a medium-high heat.

* Put one of the dough circles into the dry frying pan and cook for around 2 minutes on the first side. When you notice the bread starting to 'blister', it's time to turn it over. Flip and cook for another 2 minutes on the other side until golden and puffy.

* When cooked, immediately wrap in foil to keep warm while you make the rest. Serve the flatbreads hot with salad, a curry or meatballs.

* Once cool, these can be frozen in sealed freezer bags for up to 3 months.

# CHEAT'S NAAN BREAD

**Makes: 2 large naan breads**

Authentic naan bread can be quite tricky to make, so this recipe is actually a bit of a twist on the original, using a much simpler and more reliable method. Don't worry – it's just as tasty as the real thing! Don't miss the garlic version below, too.

125g strong white bread flour, plus extra for dusting the work surface

¼ tsp salt

¼ tsp quick-action dried yeast

½ tsp olive oil

90ml warm water (around body temperature)

Vegetable or sunflower oil, for greasing

Large baking sheet

Non-stick baking paper

For techniques in **bold** see pages 12–13.

* **Sift** the flour and salt into a large mixing bowl, add the yeast and mix well.

* Add the olive oil and warm water. Make sure the water is roughly body temperature – warm enough to activate the yeast, but not too hot to kill it. Mix well, bringing together to form a sticky ball of dough. Turn out onto a floured work surface and **knead** gently for 5 minutes.

* Place in a lightly oiled bowl and cover with cling film, ensuring the bowl is sealed, then leave in a warm place for an hour or so until the dough has doubled in size (or 'risen').

* Preheat the oven to 220°C Fan/Gas Mark 9. Grease a large baking sheet, line with non-stick baking paper and set aside.

* Sprinkle the work surface with more flour. Turn out the dough and knead gently for 2–3 minutes to bash out any air.

* Split the dough into two balls and roll out until they are around 1cm thick. Gently pull one end to stretch the dough into a teardrop shape. Make sure the dough stays flat.

* Transfer the bread dough to the prepared baking sheet and bake for 10–12 minutes, until the dough has puffed up and is lightly brown. Serve immediately.

* Once cool, these can be frozen in sealed freezer bags for up to 3 months. Defrost, then reheat in the oven for 3–5 minutes.

### GARLIC NAAN

To make a garlic version, melt 60g butter in a small saucepan over a low heat. Crush 1 large garlic clove and add to the butter. Let the garlic sit in the warm butter on a very low heat for 2–3 minutes. Drizzle the garlic butter over the breads as soon as they come out of the oven.

# BAKED
## DESSERTS

# MERINGUES

**Makes: 4 individual meringues**

Whisking up egg whites may sound scary, but meringues are actually super-easy to make. Homemade meringues have a gorgeously chewy texture that you won't find from powdery shop-bought ones. Use an electric hand whisk if you can – it makes life much easier!

**3 large egg whites**
**Pinch of salt**
**115g caster sugar**

**Large baking sheet**
**Non-stick baking paper**

For techniques in **bold** see pages 12–13.

**Tip:** To separate an egg, crack it against the side of a bowl and use your thumbs to gently pull the egg apart, making sure the yolk stays in one side of the shell and allowing the white to spill into the bowl. Then pour the yolk carefully from one shell half into the other, allowing any remaining white to spill out into the bowl. Repeat until all the egg white is in the bowl.

* Preheat the oven to 140°C Fan/Gas Mark 3. Line a large baking sheet with non-stick baking paper.

* Ensure your mixing bowl (not plastic) and whisk are spotlessly clean and completely dry before you start, as any dirt or grease will prevent the egg whites from whisking up properly.

* Place the egg whites and salt in the bowl. **Whisk** until the egg whites start to become white and foamy.

* Add the sugar a tablespoon at a time, whisking well after each addition, until stiff peaks form. The meringue will now be thick, sticky and glossy, and will stay in place when the bowl is turned upside down. (You do need to be confident it is this firm before turning the bowl over!)

* Spoon the mixture out into mounds on the baking paper. You'll need about 2 tablespoons for each meringue. Form each meringue into a round shape using the back of a spoon.

* Bake in the oven for 25 minutes, and then turn off the heat and leave it in the oven to cool completely overnight or for at least 4 hours. Try not to open the oven door during this time.

* The cooked meringues will keep for several weeks in an airtight container. Try making an Eton Mess (see below) or just fill with cream, crème fraîche or custard and top with fresh fruit, nuts or grated chocolate.

### ETON MESS

Here's a great way to use up any broken or less-than-perfect meringues. Lightly crush a meringue, keeping a few larger chunks. Place in a bowl with 50ml whipped double cream and 100g fresh berries. (If using raspberries or blueberries, add them whole; if using strawberries, cut into quarters.) Add 2–3 tablespoons of sifted icing sugar, mix everything well and serve immediately. These quantities serve one: for more people, simply multiply.

# FRUIT PAVLOVA

**Serves: 8**

This is ideal for a barbecue or summer dessert, and you may be surprised how quick and easy it is to make. You can prepare the meringue well in advance and wrap in baking paper and foil to keep it fresh until needed (it keeps for several weeks). An electric whisk is very helpful here, although not essential.

### For the meringue
4 large egg whites
Pinch of salt
230g caster sugar

### For the topping
400ml double cream
800g mixed fruit of your choice
e.g. berries, banana, mango,
passion fruit, peaches
3 tbsp icing sugar, for dusting

Large baking sheet
Non-stick baking paper

For techniques in **bold**
see pages 12–13.

* Preheat the oven to 140°C Fan/Gas Mark 3.

* Line a large baking sheet with non-stick baking paper. Place a cake tin of roughly 20cm diameter onto the baking paper and draw around it. This will be a guide to help you shape the meringue neatly. Set the baking sheet aside.

* Ensure your mixing bowl (not plastic) and whisk are spotlessly clean and completely dry before you start the next step, as any dirt or grease will prevent the egg whites from whisking up properly.

* Place the egg whites and pinch of salt in the mixing bowl. **Whisk** until the egg whites start to become white and foamy. Now add the caster sugar a tablespoon at a time, whisking well after each addition, until stiff peaks form. The meringue will be thick, sticky and glossy, and will stay in place when the bowl is turned upside down. (You do need to be confident it is this firm before turning the bowl over!)

* Turn the meringue out into the centre of the circle and spread it out evenly to form a large round shape. Try to create a well in the centre, which will hold the fruit and cream, but make sure the well isn't too deep.

* Bake the pavlova in the oven for 45 minutes, then turn off the heat and leave it in the oven to cool completely overnight, or for at least 4 hours. Try not to open the oven door during this time.

* Just before you are ready to serve, whisk the cream in a bowl until firm. Spread it over the meringue and top with fresh fruit.

* Finish by **sifting** a light dusting of icing sugar over the top and serve immediately.

# FRUITY BAKED MERINGUE

**Serves: 4**

This is a super-simple yet very impressive pudding, ideal to feed to friends. It consists of delicious warm fruit topped with a soft cloud of sweet meringue. Choose the best and freshest fruit available.

**3 peaches, halved and stones removed**

**100g raspberries (fresh or frozen and defrosted)**

**35g light brown soft sugar**

**2 tsp vanilla extract**

**2 large egg whites**

**190g caster sugar**

**Ovenproof dish, 1.5-litre capacity**

For techniques in **bold** see pages 12–13.

* Preheat the oven to 180°C Fan/Gas Mark 6.

* Place the peaches into a large ovenproof dish, skin-side down. Scatter the raspberries evenly around the peaches.

* Sprinkle over the brown sugar and drizzle with the vanilla extract. Set aside.

* Ensure your mixing bowl (not plastic) and whisk are spotlessly clean and completely dry before you start the next step, as any dirt or grease will prevent the egg whites from whisking up properly.

* Place the egg whites into the mixing bowl. **Whisk** until they start to become white and foamy. If you have an electric whisk, it is very helpful here.

* Add the caster sugar a tablespoon at a time, whisking well after each addition, until stiff peaks form. The meringue will now be thick, sticky and glossy, and will stay in place when the bowl is turned upside down. (You do need to be confident it is this firm before turning the bowl over!)

* Gently spoon the meringue over the fruit and, using a knife or spatula, add a few decorative swirls to give it some texture.

* Bake in the oven for 20–25 minutes until the meringue is really golden brown and feels firmly set in the centre. Give it a gentle poke with your finger to test. Serve immediately.

# LEMON MERINGUE PIE

Serves: 6–8

A homemade lemon meringue pie looks and tastes amazing, but can involve quite a lot of work if done from scratch. So this version cheats a bit by using ready-made pastry and shop-bought lemon curd. It's still totally delicious, but much quicker and easier to make.

Vegetable oil or butter, for greasing

200–250g ready-made, ready-rolled sweet shortcrust pastry, fridge-cold

325g jar lemon curd

3 tbsp cornflour

3 large egg whites

150g caster sugar

20cm pie or flan dish (or round springform cake tin)

Non-stick baking paper

Baking beans (see page 8)

For techniques in **bold** see pages 12–13.

* Preheat the oven to 200°C Fan/Gas Mark 7. Grease a 20cm pie or flan dish (or round springform cake tin) and line with non-stick baking paper.

* Unwrap the pastry and lower the sheet into the dish. Press gently into the sides of the dish and trim the excess from around the edges. Save the excess pastry for something else.

* Prick the pastry base all over with a fork and cover with non-stick baking paper. Fill with baking beans, or dried lentils or beans, pushing them right up to the edges. Bake the pastry case for 15 minutes, then remove the beans and paper and cook for a further 5 minutes until it feels crisp and has just started to brown in places. Set aside to cool for 30 minutes.

* Place the lemon curd in a small saucepan, add the cornflour and stir in well. Over a medium heat, continue to stir the curd until it starts to bubble gently. Keep stirring continuously for around 3 minutes until the curd is thickened.

* When the pastry case has cooled, pour the lemon curd into the middle and spread out evenly inside the pastry case.

* Ensure your mixing bowl (not plastic) and whisk are spotlessly clean and completely dry before the next step, as any dirt or grease will prevent the egg whites from whisking up properly.

* Place the egg whites into the bowl and **whisk** until white and foamy. An electric whisk is very helpful here. Then add the sugar a tablespoon at a time, whisking well after each addition, until stiff peaks form. It will now be thick, sticky and glossy, and will stay in place when the bowl is turned upside down.

* Gently spoon the meringue over the lemon curd and make a few decorative swirls on top. Bake in the oven for 20 minutes until the meringue is lightly golden brown and feels set. Poke it gently with your finger to test. Allow to cool before serving.

# FRUIT COBBLER

**Serves: 6**

The name of this old-fashioned pud comes from its appearance – because the topping resembles street cobbles. It can be made with many different types of fruit, including apples, plums, peaches and berries. Choose your favourite.

## For the fruit

800g fruit, washed, stoned and halved, or peeled, cored and sliced, as appropriate

80g caster sugar

## For the cobbles

220g self-raising flour, plus extra for the work surface

Pinch of salt

35g caster sugar

55g butter, chilled and cubed

150ml milk, plus extra for brushing

Icing sugar, for dusting

Ovenproof dish, 1.5-litre capacity

Rolling pin (or wine bottle)

Round cookie cutter (or glass)

For techniques in **bold** see pages 12–13.

* Preheat the oven to 180°C Fan/Gas Mark 6.

* Place the fruit into a large ovenproof dish, about 1.5 litres in capacity, sprinkle with the sugar and set aside.

* Now make the cobbles. **Sift** the flour into a large mixing bowl, add the salt and sugar and stir in so they are evenly mixed.

* Add the butter to the bowl and rub into the other ingredients with your fingertips until the mixture looks like breadcrumbs.

* Pour in the milk and gently stir in. The mixture will start to come together to form a soft dough.

* Now use your hands to bring the dough together into a ball, taking care to handle the dough gently.

* Make sure the work surface is clean and then sprinkle well with flour.

* Tip the dough out onto the floured surface and **knead** very gently for a minute.

* Using a rolling pin or clean wine bottle, roll out the dough to 2.5cm thick and cut out your cobbles with a cookie cutter or clean drinking glass. They can be any size you like.

* Arrange the cobbles close to each other on top of the fruit. Brush with the extra milk and bake for 30–40 minutes until the cobbles are golden brown and the fruit underneath is soft and bubbling.

* Dust with icing sugar, and serve hot with cream, custard or ice cream.

# APPLE PIE

Serves: 6–8

Who doesn't love homemade apple pie? It's perfect after a Sunday roast, but your friends will thank you anytime! It tastes amazing served hot or cold with ice cream or custard.

### For the apple filling

650g eating apples, peeled, cored and cut into slices

70g caster sugar

1 tsp ground cinnamon

4 tsp water

### For the pastry

300g plain flour, **sifted**

150g butter, cubed and chilled

4 tsp caster sugar, plus 3 tbsp for sprinkling

2 large egg yolks, and 1 large egg, beaten, for glazing

2½ tbsp ice-cold water

Vegetable oil or butter, for greasing

20cm pie dish, flan tin or round springform cake tin

**Tip:** Eating apples work fine in this pie, but feel free to use cooking apples, such as Bramleys, adding an extra heaped tablespoon of sugar if so. If you don't fancy making the pastry, you can use a 375g pack of ready-made sweet shortcrust pastry.

* Place the apple slices in a saucepan with the sugar, cinnamon and water, and cook over a medium heat for 10 minutes. The apples should soften a little during this time. Set aside to cool.

* Place the flour and butter for the pastry into a mixing bowl. Rub together lightly using your fingers until the mixture resembles breadcrumbs.

* Add the sugar and egg yolks, and stir into the butter and flour. Finally, add the cold water, a little at a time. Use a table knife to stir it into the mixture.

* Once the water has been added, bring the pastry together into a ball. Wrap in cling film and chill in the fridge for 20 minutes.

* While the pastry is chilling, preheat the oven to 200°C Fan/Gas Mark 7. Grease a 20cm pie dish, flan tin or round springform cake tin well and set aside.

* When the pastry is chilled, break off half of the ball and place it between two large sheets of cling film. Roll out until large enough to fit the dish; it should be around 3–5mm in thickness.

* Fit the pastry into the dish and press it into the edges and round the sides. If you are using a springform cake tin, build the pastry up to 5cm around the edges and trim neatly. If you are using the pie dish, leave 1–2cm excess pastry around the rim. If you have any thin patches, just press some excess pastry over them to cover them up.

* Fill the pastry case with the cooled apple mixture.

* Roll out the second half of the pastry as you did the first half. Dab a little cold water onto the edges of the pastry that's

already in the tin, then place the second piece of pastry on top and press down gently around the sides to seal.

* Trim around the edges using a sharp knife, then use a fork to press down all around the rim of the pie, which will seal the pastry further and create a decorative effect.

* Brush the pie with the beaten egg to glaze, and sprinkle with the extra caster sugar. Make a couple of cuts in the centre of the pie using a sharp knife.

* Bake the pie for 25–30 minutes until the pastry is crisp and golden brown and any visible filling is bubbling. Serve with cream, custard or ice cream.

# APPLE AND SULTANA STRUDEL

**Serves: 6**

This traditional Austrian pud is the ultimate winter comfort food. It's the perfect follow-up to a Sunday lunch, and bound to warm the heart! Serve hot with cream or ice cream.

5 small eating apples, peeled, cored and cut into 1cm cubes

Juice of ½ lemon

100g sultanas

Pinch of ground cinnamon

150g light brown soft sugar

Vegetable oil or butter, for greasing

200g ready-made, ready-rolled puff pastry, fridge-cold

2 tsp milk

Large baking sheet

Non-stick baking paper

* Preheat the oven to 180°C Fan/Gas Mark 6.

* Place the apple cubes, lemon juice, sultanas, cinnamon and sugar in a large bowl and stir together well. Set aside.

* Grease a large baking sheet well and line with non-stick baking paper. Lay out the sheet of puff pastry carefully on it.

* Spoon out the apple mixture along one edge of the pastry, running about 3cm away from the edge (see pictures overleaf).

* Once you have created an even line of fruit along the pastry, tightly roll up the pastry from one of the long sides with the fruit in the centre, like a Swiss roll.

* When you have rolled up the pastry, squeeze it together gently and press down on the seam to make sure it is sealed. Fold up the ends well and press together to seal.

* Lay the strudel with the pastry seam underneath. Brush with milk and make a few slits in the pastry on the top.

* Bake for 25–30 minutes until golden brown and the pastry is crisp. Serve warm or cold, with cream or ice cream.

# PEAR, DATE AND GINGER STRUDEL

**Serves: 6**

Here's another strudel recipe, this time with slightly fancier ingredients – but just as easy to make. Dates are delicious when baked, giving a rich toffee flavour to the strudel, and the fresh ginger adds a spicy kick and a little warmth.

4 small pears, peeled, cored and cut into 1cm cubes

100g dates, stones removed and chopped

2 tsp peeled and finely grated fresh root ginger

100g light brown soft sugar

Vegetable oil or butter, for greasing

200g ready-made, ready-rolled puff pastry, fridge-cold

2 tbsp milk

Large baking sheet
Non-stick baking paper

* Preheat the oven to 180°C Fan/Gas Mark 6.

* Place the cubes of pear, date pieces, ginger and sugar in a large bowl and stir together well. Set aside.

* Grease a large baking sheet well, line with non-stick baking paper and set out your sheet of puff pastry carefully on it.

* Spoon out the pear mixture along one edge of the pastry, running about 3cm away from the edge.

* Once you have created an even line of fruit along the pastry, tightly roll up the pastry from one long side with the fruit in the centre, like a Swiss roll.

* When you have rolled up the pastry, squeeze it together gently and press down on the seam to make sure it is sealed. Fold up the ends well and press together to seal.

* Lay the strudel with the pastry seam underneath. Brush with milk and make a few slits in the pastry on the top.

* Bake for 25–30 minutes until golden brown and the pastry is crisp. Serve warm or cold, with cream or ice cream.

# APPLE AND SUMMER BERRY GALETTE

**Serves: 6–8**

A simple combination of ready-made pastry and warm fruit, this is probably one of the easiest and prettiest desserts you'll ever make. Fresh berries are best of course, but if you're on a shoestring budget, or making this in winter, bags of frozen berries can be picked up cheaply in the supermarket freezer aisle.

Vegetable oil or butter, for greasing

375g pack of ready-made, ready-rolled puff pastry, fridge-cold

40g ground almonds

400g eating apples, cored and sliced very thinly

200g summer berries (fresh or frozen and defrosted, with excess juice discarded)

1 large egg, beaten

6 tbsp demerara sugar

Icing sugar, for dusting

Large baking sheet
Non-stick baking paper

* Preheat the oven to 200°C Fan/Gas Mark 7.

* Grease a large baking sheet well and line with non-stick baking paper. Lay out the sheet of puff pastry carefully on it.

* Sprinkle the ground almonds evenly over the centre of the pastry sheet, leaving about 4cm around the edges.

* Lay the slices of apple neatly over the almonds and scatter the berries over the top.

* Fold up the corners and press the pastry together. The edges should cover the fruit slightly, but give structure to the sides of the galette.

* Brush the pastry generously with the beaten egg and sprinkle 4 tablespoons of demerara sugar over the fruit, and the remaining 2 tablespoons of sugar over the pastry.

* Bake for 25–30 minutes until the fruit is soft and the pastry is golden. Dust with icing sugar, if you like and serve warm with cream or ice cream.

**Tip:** For a delicious autumnal version of this recipe, try using pears and blackberries.

# TREACLE TART

**Serves: 6**

A much-loved British classic, this traditional tart is ideal if you have a sweet tooth. Rather than buying ready-made breadcrumbs, it's cheaper to save stale white bread and whiz it up into crumbs, then keep them in a food bag or Tupperware container in the freezer until needed.

Butter, for greasing

375g pack of ready-made, ready-rolled shortcrust pastry (not sweet shortcrust), fridge-cold

240g golden syrup

Finely grated zest of 1 lemon, plus 75ml lemon juice (from approx. 1–2 lemons)

150g fresh white breadcrumbs

Plain flour, for dusting

1 medium egg, beaten

20cm round springform cake tin (or pie dish)

Non-stick baking paper

Baking beans (see page 8)

* Preheat the oven to 190°C Fan/Gas Mark 6. Grease a 20cm round springform cake tin (or pie dish) well with butter.

* Unwrap the pastry and lower the sheet into the tin. Press into the edges to fit the tin and build the sides up to about 3cm tall. Trim around the edges neatly. Retain the excess pastry.

* Prick the pastry all over the base with a fork and cover with a layer of non-stick baking paper. Fill the pastry case with baking beans or dried lentils or beans, taking care to push them right up to the edges. Bake the pastry case for 15 minutes, then remove the paper and beans or lentils and bake for a further 5–8 minutes until it feels crisp and has just started to brown in places.

* In a large mixing bowl, combine the golden syrup, lemon zest and juice. Stir together well. Add the breadcrumbs and stir in. Tip this mixture into the pastry case and spread out.

* Roll out the pastry trimmings on a clean, well-floured work surface, and cut into strips that are 20cm long and 1cm wide.

* Lay the strips across the top of the pie in a lattice pattern. Be careful not to stretch the pastry across the tart, as it will shrink back when it cooks. Trim any excess pastry from the edges and discard or save for something else.

* Brush the pastry lattice with beaten egg and bake for 25–35 minutes until the pastry and filling are both golden. Cut into slices and serve with ice cream, custard or cream.

# SPICED BAKED RICE PUDDING

**Serves: 4**

This is a soft and creamy pudding with a delicious hint of spice. If you have leftovers, this keeps for up to 3 days in the fridge and can be reheated easily. It's also delicious cold. Make sure to buy proper pudding rice as other types don't work here.

Butter, for greasing

100g pudding rice

700ml full-fat milk

200ml double cream

50g caster sugar

2 cardamom pods, crushed

Generous pinch of ground cinnamon

Generous pinch of ground nutmeg

1 tsp vanilla extract

Ovenproof dish, 1-litre capacity

* Preheat the oven to 140°C Fan/Gas Mark 3. Grease a 1-litre ovenproof dish well with butter.

* Place the rice, milk, cream, sugar, spices and vanilla extract into the dish and stir together well.

* Bake for 1 hour 20 minutes–1 hour 30 minutes, until the rice is cooked through and tender, and there is a crust on top. Serve hot or cold.

# PEAR TARTE TATIN

**Serves: 4–6**

A bit like an upside-down pie, this gorgeous dessert really does have the wow factor, and is ideal for feeding friends or impressing parents when they visit. Don't be put off by the fancy name – like everything else in this book it's not tricky to make.

50g butter, plus extra
for greasing

50g caster sugar

1 tsp vanilla extract

3 large ripe pears,
peeled, halved and cored

200–250g ready-made,
ready-rolled puff pastry,
fridge-cold

20cm round springform cake tin

Large baking sheet

* Preheat the oven to 200°C Fan/Gas Mark 7. Grease a 20cm round springform cake tin with butter.

* Place the butter and sugar in a large frying pan. Melt the butter over a low heat and then turn the temperature up to high, allowing the mixture to bubble away until it turns brown in colour and begins to thicken. This is called caramelising. Turn the heat right down as soon as the sugar begins to caramelise because it can easily burn. Add the vanilla extract and stir into the caramel.

* Add the pears to the caramel, cut-side facing up, and cook in the caramel sauce very gently over a low heat for 10 minutes. Spoon the caramel over the pears while they are cooking.

* Arrange the pears, again cut-side up, in the bottom of the cake tin and pour the caramel over the top of them.

* Lay out the puff pastry and cut out a circle to fit in the tin. Place the pastry over the pears and tuck the excess pastry around inside the tin. Prick the pastry a couple of times on the top using a sharp knife.

* Place the cake tin on a baking sheet and bake the tarte in the oven for 25–30 minutes until the pastry is golden brown.

* Leave the tarte to rest for 5 minutes in the tin before removing the sides of the tin. You may wish to run a sharp knife around the edges first.

* Now, place a plate over the tarte and flip it over to turn the tarte out onto the plate. Remove the base of the cake tin and serve the tarte immediately with cream or ice cream.

# BAKED LEMON PUDDING

Serves: 4

This is a totally fuss-free pudding. It's zesty and full of flavour, and delicious served with ice cream.

75g butter, plus a little extra for the dish

275g caster sugar

Grated zest of 1 lemon

2 medium eggs, beaten

90ml lemon juice

300ml milk

60g self-raising flour

1 tsp baking powder

Ovenproof dish, about 1-litre capacity

For techniques in **bold** see pages 12–13.

* Preheat the oven to 180°C Fan/Gas Mark 6.

* Grease a 1 litre-capacity ovenproof baking dish with butter and set aside.

* Place the butter, sugar and lemon zest into a bowl and **beat** together until well combined.

* Add the beaten eggs and mix together well, followed by the lemon juice and milk.

* **Sift** in the flour and baking powder and stir together to form a runny batter.

* Pour the mixture into the prepared dish and bake for 40–50 minutes until sponge-like on top and crisp around the edges. Serve hot or cold.

# SPICED PEAR CRUMBLE

Serves: 6

A classic fruit crumble is one of the cheapest and simplest puds you can make. This spiced pear filling is a delicious twist on the more usual apple mixture – go on, be adventurous!

### For the filling

900g pears, peeled, cored and chopped into 2cm cubes

50g light brown soft sugar

1 tsp ground cinnamon

4 cardamom pods, cut open and seeds extracted and retained

### For the topping

100g plain flour

50g butter, chilled and cubed

50g light brown soft sugar

50g porridge oats

Ovenproof dish, 1.5-litre capacity

* Preheat the oven to 180°C Fan/Gas Mark 6.

* For the filling, place the pears, sugar, cinnamon and cardamom seeds in a 1.5-litre ovenproof dish and stir together to combine.

* In a mixing bowl, rub together the flour and butter with your fingertips until they resemble breadcrumbs.

* Stir in the sugar and oats, and then sprinkle the crumble topping evenly over the pears in the dish.

* Bake for 30–40 minutes until the crumble topping is golden brown and the fruit is soft and bubbling up the sides. Serve hot with cream, ice cream or custard.

# BERRY AND APPLE CRUMBLE

Serves: 4

Crumbles are simple and cheap to make, and are ideal for feeding larger groups, perhaps after a Sunday lunch. Here's a fairly traditional filling flavour, or see page 203 for a more unusual spiced pear version.

## For the fruit

400g apples, peeled, cored and sliced

400g berries (any type you like)

30g demerara sugar

## For the crumble topping

100g plain flour

65g butter, chilled and cubed

50g demerara sugar

50g porridge oats

Ovenproof dish, 1.5-litre capacity

* Preheat the oven to 200°C Fan/Gas Mark 7.

* Place the prepared apples and berries in the bottom of a 1.5-litre ovenproof dish. Sprinkle the demerara sugar evenly over the fruit.

* To make the crumble topping, place the flour and butter into a bowl. Rub together using your fingertips until the mixture looks like breadcrumbs.

* Add the sugar and oats and stir into the mixture. Sprinkle the crumble topping evenly over the fruit.

* Bake for 30–40 minutes until the crumble topping is golden brown and the fruit is soft and bubbling up the sides. Serve hot with cream, ice cream or custard.

**Tip:** You can use fresh or frozen berries here. It's a good way to use up any berries that are past their prime.

# STICKY TOFFEE PUDDING

**Serves: 6–8**

This fantastically sweet British pudding is a cinch to make yourself, and your friends are bound to love you for it!

## For the pudding

150g dates, without stones, chopped

1 tsp bicarbonate of soda

275ml boiling water

40g butter, softened

150g caster sugar

2 medium eggs, beaten

1 tsp vanilla extract

150g self-raising flour

## For the sauce

275ml double cream

1 tbsp treacle

50g dark brown soft sugar

Ovenproof dish,
1.5-litre capacity

For techniques in **bold**
see pages 12–13.

* Place the dates into a heatproof bowl. Add the bicarbonate of soda and pour over the boiling water. Leave the dates to soften for at least an hour (or overnight if time allows).

* Preheat the oven to 180°C Fan/Gas mark 6.

* In a large mixing bowl, **beat** together the butter and sugar until pale and fluffy. This will take a few minutes as there is quite a lot of sugar.

* Add the beaten eggs, a little at a time, beating well after each addition. Add the vanilla extract and stir in.

* **Sift** in the flour and stir in well. Now, tip in the dates and their liquid.

* Transfer the mixture into a 1.5-litre ovenproof dish. Bake in the oven for 30-35 minutes until firm.

* To make the sauce, put the cream, treacle and brown sugar together in a saucepan over a medium heat. Stir together well and allow the mixture to bubble for around 10 minutes. Preheat the grill to a high temperature.

* Once the pudding is cooked, pour over the sauce and grill until it bubbles slightly around the edge, taking care that the topping does not brown.

* Remove from the grill, cut up the pudding into portions and serve, ideally with vanilla ice cream.

# CHOCOLATE MOUSSE PUDDING

**Serves: 6**

Incredibly rich yet light, this pudding has a mousse centre and a firm top a bit like a brownie. If you're lucky, you sometimes get a delicious chocolatey sauce at the bottom of the dish, hiding under the mousse.

**150g butter, plus extra for greasing**

**150g dark chocolate, broken into squares**

**1 tsp vanilla extract**

**150ml hot water**

**125g caster sugar**

**4 medium eggs**

**1 tbsp plain flour, sifted**

**½ tsp baking powder**

**Ovenproof dish, 1.5-litre capacity**

**Large roasting tray**

For techniques in **bold** see pages 12–13.

* Preheat the oven to 160°C/Gas Mark 4. Grease a 1.5-litre ovenproof dish with butter. Place this inside a large roasting tray or larger ovenproof dish with tall sides and set aside.

* Melt the butter and chocolate together. You can do this in a non-metallic bowl in the microwave (make sure you check it every 20 seconds so that it does not burn) or in a heatproof bowl set over a small saucepan of simmering water (stir frequently and check the water isn't actually in contact with the bottom of the bowl).

* When the chocolate and butter are melted, mix vigorously to combine. Set aside and allow to cool for 10 minutes or so.

* Stir the vanilla, hot water and sugar into the chocolate and butter mixture.

* Separate the eggs (see Tip on page 181) and **whisk** the egg whites until they are stiff. An electric whisk is very helpful for this. When stiff enough, they will be thick, sticky and glossy.

* Add the egg yolks, flour and baking powder to the chocolate mixture and gently stir in.

* **Fold** the egg whites into the chocolate mix, being very gentle so that you don't knock out the air. Keep folding until there are no large lumps of egg white remaining. Now boil the kettle.

* Pour the chocolate mixture into the buttered dish and fill the outer tray or dish with around 3–5cm of boiling water, depending on its size, so that the water comes about halfway up the exterior of the smaller pudding dish.

* Bake for 20–30 minutes until a pale-brown crust has formed on top and it feels firm to the touch (it will still be soft inside). Remove the pudding dish from the outer tray, carefully give it a wipe, and serve immediately.

# BANOFFEE PIE

Serves: 6–8

Homemade banoffee pie looks impressive, but is a doddle to make. It takes just minutes to put together and you can then leave it to chill until you're ready to serve. Canned caramel can be found in larger supermarkets near the condensed milk.

**Vegetable oil or butter, for greasing**

**250g digestive biscuits**

**100g butter, melted**

**400g tin of canned caramel**

**3 bananas**

**300ml double cream**

**1 tbsp cocoa powder, for dusting**

**20cm round springform cake tin**

For techniques in **bold** see pages 12–13.

* Lightly grease a 20cm round springform cake tin and set aside.

* Place the biscuits in a large plastic freezer bag, flatten to remove as much air as possible and knot the top. Bash using a rolling pin or similar implement until the biscuits resemble powder. Don't use anything sharp that might pierce the bag.

* Empty the biscuit crumbs into a mixing bowl and stir in the melted butter. Tip this mixture into your prepared tin and press down evenly to cover the base of the tin. Build the topping up the sides to about 3cm high to form a biscuit shell to hold the filling. Chill in the fridge for 2 hours.

* Once the biscuit base has chilled, pour the canned caramel onto it and spread it out in an even layer.

* Slice the bananas and lay them out on top of the caramel.

* Finally, **whisk** the double cream until it forms soft peaks and spread it evenly on top of the bananas. Chill the pie in the fridge for an hour or two before removing from the tin, dusting lightly with cocoa powder and serving.

# BAKED LEMON CHEESECAKE

Serves: 8

This is a very simple, classic cheesecake recipe. It's light, creamy, zesty and very moreish.

**For the base**

225g digestive biscuits

85g butter, melted, plus extra for greasing

**For the topping**

800g full-fat cream cheese

350g caster sugar

3 large eggs, beaten

1 tsp vanilla extract

1 tbsp plain flour

Finely grated zest and juice of 2 lemons

20cm round springform cake tin

For techniques in **bold** see pages 12–3.

* Preheat the oven to 180°C Fan/Gas Mark 6. Grease a 20cm round springform cake tin well and set aside.

* Place the digestive biscuits in a large plastic freezer bag, flatten to remove as much air as possible and knot the top. Bash with a rolling pin or similar implement until the biscuits resemble powder. Don't use anything sharp that might pierce the bag.

* Empty the biscuit crumbs into a mixing bowl and stir in the melted butter. Tip the buttery biscuit crumbs into the prepared tin and press down to form a flat base. Ensure that the base is level and not raised at the edges. Set aside.

* Add the cream cheese, sugar, eggs and vanilla to a large mixing bowl and **beat** together well. If you have an electric whisk, it will speed up this step considerably. Ensure there are no lumps in the mixture.

* Add the flour, lemon juice and zest and stir through well.

* Spoon the cheesecake mixture into the tin on top of the digestive base and even out using a spatula or the back of a spoon.

* Bake the cheesecake for 55–65 minutes until the centre is still very slightly wobbly. Leave in the tin without touching the cheesecake until it is completely cool. Cover with cling film and refrigerate overnight before removing from the tin and serving in slices.

# NO-BAKE CHOCOLATE CHEESECAKE

Serves: 8–10

This recipe makes a milk chocolate cheesecake. If you prefer your chocolate a bit stronger, just use dark chocolate and dark chocolate biscuits. This is a very easy cheesecake to make, with the added bonus of not even needing the oven!

**For the base**

12 milk chocolate
digestive biscuits

80g butter, melted,
plus extra for greasing

**For the topping**

200g milk chocolate, chopped

400g full-fat cream cheese

300ml double cream

100g icing sugar, **sifted**

20cm round springform
cake tin

For techniques in **bold**
see pages 12–13.

* Start by making the base. Lightly grease a 20cm round springform cake tin and set aside.

* Place the biscuits in a large plastic freezer bag, flatten to remove as much air as possible and knot the top. Bash with a rolling pin or similar implement until the biscuits resemble powder. Don't use anything sharp that might pierce the bag.

* Empty the biscuit crumbs into a mixing bowl and stir in the melted butter. Tip this mixture into your prepared tin and flatten it down evenly to cover the base of the tin. Set aside.

* Melt half the chocolate. You can do this in a non-metallic bowl in the microwave (make sure you check it every 20 seconds so that it does not burn) or in a heatproof bowl over a small saucepan of simmering water (stir frequently and check the water isn't actually in contact with the bottom of the bowl).

* Once the chocolate is melted, allow to cool for 10 minutes or so before using. Keep stirring so that the chocolate does not solidify again.

* Place the cream cheese in a large bowl and **beat** well. **Whisk** the double cream in another large bowl until it is stiff, then add it to the cream cheese along with the **sifted** icing sugar. Stir together gently.

* Finally, add the cooled melted chocolate and remaining chopped chocolate and stir in gently. Stir as little as possible to retain a lovely swirled effect.

* Gently spoon the cheesecake mixture into the tin on top of the biscuit base and make sure the top is even and smooth. Chill for at least 4 hours, or overnight, before removing from the tin and serving in slices.

# STRAWBERRY DAIQUIRI CHEESECAKE

Serves: 8

Inspired by the famous cocktail, this boozy no-bake cheesecake is super-easy and is great to serve at a party. Why not use the rest of the bottle of rum for cocktails?

### For the base

12 digestive biscuits

80g butter, melted, plus extra for greasing

### For the strawberry filling

350g strawberries, hulled and sliced lengthways

2 heaped tbsp caster sugar

3 tbsp white rum

Finely grated zest of 1 lime

### For the cheesecake mixture

350ml double cream

350g mascarpone cheese

100ml soured cream

75g caster sugar

½ tsp vanilla extract

### For the topping

100g strawberries, hulled and sliced lengthways

20cm round springform cake tin

For techniques in **bold** see pages 12–13.

* Start by making the base. Lightly grease a 20cm round springform cake tin and set aside.

* Place the biscuits in a large plastic freezer bag, flatten to remove as much air as possible and knot the top. Bash using a rolling pin or similar implement until the biscuits resemble powder. Don't use anything sharp that might pierce the bag.

* Empty the biscuit crumbs into a mixing bowl and stir in the melted butter. Tip this mixture into your prepared tin and flatten it down evenly to cover the base of the tin. Set aside.

* Place the 350g strawberries for the filling into a bowl along with the sugar, rum and lime zest. Stir well and leave for 1 hour to allow the strawberries to soak up the flavours.

* To make the cheesecake mixture, **whisk** the double cream until it forms soft peaks. Add the mascarpone cheese, soured cream, caster sugar and vanilla extract, and whisk all the ingredients until evenly mixed and smooth.

* Drain the soaked strawberries through a sieve (keeping the rum for a cocktail!), and then lay the strawberries out evenly over the cheesecake base.

* Spoon over the cheesecake mixture and level out with the back of the spoon. Cover with cling film and chill for 6 hours.

* To remove the cheesecake from the tin, run a thin knife or palette knife around the edges, being very careful not to scratch your tin if non-stick. Then remove the side piece of the tin and place the cheesecake onto a plate. Don't worry about removing the base of the tin.

* Decorate the top of the cheesecake with the remaining strawberries and serve immediately.

# CHERRY AND ALMOND PUDDING

**Serves: 4 generously**

Simple to make but stunning to eat, this is a surefire way to wow your friends with not much effort required. Make it in advance if you can, as this actually tastes better the day after it's been cooked. Reheat if you wish. Save some for leftovers for the same reason.

Vegetable oil or butter, for greasing

400g cherries, stoned

150g butter, softened

150g caster sugar

2 large eggs, beaten

150g ground almonds

1 tsp vanilla extract (optional)

2 tbsp flaked almonds (optional)

Ovenproof dish, 1.5-litre capacity (or 23cm square cake tin)

For techniques in **bold** see pages 12–13.

**Tip:** This is a great way to use up any fresh cherries that are past their prime. But if you can't afford or get hold of fresh cherries, it's also fine to use stoned cherries from a jar or tin, but drain them first.

* Preheat the oven to 180°C Fan/Gas Mark 6. Grease an ovenproof dish, about 1.5 litres in capacity, or a 23cm square cake tin. Set aside.

* If you are using cherries from a tin or a jar, drain them well. If you need to remove the stones from fresh cherries, do so now.

* Place the prepared cherries in the baking dish or tin, so that they cover the base evenly. Set aside.

* In a mixing bowl, **beat** together the butter and sugar until pale and fluffy.

* In a small bowl, **whisk** the eggs. Add them a little at a time to the butter and sugar mixture, beating well after each addition.

* Add the ground almonds and stir in. You should now have a thick mixture, like cake batter. If you are using the vanilla extract, add this to the mixture now and stir in.

* Dollop the mixture, a tablespoon at a time, evenly over the cherries. Smooth over with a spoon to create an even finish.

* If you fancy topping the pudding with some extra flaked almonds, scatter them over now.

* Place the pudding in the oven to cook for about 30 minutes until the sponge is golden brown.

* Enjoy this pudding hot or cold, with custard, cream, yoghurt or ice cream.

# CHOCOLATE AND PEAR TORTE

Serves: 8

This is a moist, flourless cake made with ground almonds. Don't expect it to rise like a sponge cake – it's very rich with an indulgent mousse-like texture. It makes a sophisticated dessert, dusted with icing sugar if you wish. See picture overleaf.

Vegetable oil or butter, for greasing

125g dark chocolate, broken into squares

125g butter

4 medium eggs

125g caster sugar

125g ground almonds

1 tbsp strong coffee

5 ripe pears, peeled, cored and halved

Icing sugar (optional), for dusting

20cm round springform cake tin

Non-stick baking paper

For techniques in **bold** see pages 12–13.

* Preheat the oven to 180°C Fan/Gas Mark 6. Grease a 20cm round springform cake tin, line with non-stick baking paper and set aside.

* Start by melting the chocolate and butter together. You can do this in a non-metallic bowl in the microwave (make sure you check it every 20 seconds so that it does not burn) or in a heatproof bowl over a small saucepan of simmering water (stir frequently and check the water isn't actually in contact with the bottom of the bowl).

* When the chocolate and butter are melted, mix vigorously to combine. Set aside and allow to cool for 10 minutes or so.

* Now, separate the egg yolks from the egg whites into different bowls (see Tip on page 181).

* Add the sugar to the egg whites and **whisk** vigorously until stiff. An electric whisk is very helpful for this. When stiff enough, they will be thick, sticky and glossy.

* Stir the whisked egg whites, yolks, almonds and coffee gently into the cooled melted chocolate and butter.

* Lay out the pears, cut-side down, in the base of the prepared tin. Gently spoon over the topping and even out with a spatula or the back of a spoon.

* Bake for 45 minutes. Allow to cool completely before removing from the tin, as the torte will be fragile.

# PEACH CRISP

**Serves: 4–6**

A bit like a crumble, but with a bread topping, this is a very easy and economical pudding to make and a great way to use up stale bread. If you can't get hold of peaches it's also really good made with plums.

**8 peaches, halved and stones removed**

**50g light brown soft sugar**

**8 slices stale white bread, crusts removed and cut into squares**

**60g caster sugar**

**110g butter, melted**

**2 tsp ground cinnamon**

**Pinch of ground cloves**

Ovenproof dish,
1.5-litre capacity
(or 24cm round pie dish)

For techniques in **bold** see pages 12–13.

* Preheat the oven to 170°C Fan/Gas Mark 5.

* Place the peaches flat-side down in a 1.5-litre ovenproof dish or 24cm pie dish and sprinkle them with the brown sugar.

* Layer your squares of bread attractively over the top of the peaches.

* Add the caster sugar to the melted butter, along with the cinnamon and cloves, and **whisk** together well.

* Drizzle the butter evenly over the bread so that it is all covered.

* Bake for 40–45 minutes until the bread is golden brown and the peaches are soft and bubbling. Serve the pudding hot or cold with ice cream.

**Tip:** This is a great way to use up any stubborn peaches that refuse to ripen, although ripe ones are also perfectly good here too. Or for those on a tight budget, canned peaches also work very well.

# INDEX

Page numbers in **bold**
denote an illustration

# AUTHOR'S
# ACKNOWLEDGEMENTS

Thank you to my fantastic agent, Clare Hulton, for seeing something in me, and for all your support, guidance and answers to my numerous questions.

Sincerest thanks to Jenny Heller at Quercus for your vision, enthusiasm and backing. It is a great pleasure and privilege to work with you. Thank you to Ione Walder for so expertly guiding me through every step and for being a complete and utter joy to work with, and thanks indeed to everyone at Quercus for all your hard work. Caroline and Clive at Harris + Wilson, Jonathan Cherry and Lincoln Jefferson, thank you for a brilliant photo shoot, and for being such fun to work with. Thanks also to A-Side studio for your great design and layout.

Many thanks are due to every single member of my testing team for going above and beyond to triple-test each recipe. I'm also lucky to have so many wonderful friends who haven't forgotten me despite how elusive I've been over the last couple of years. Thanks for sticking with me and for your constant support. Thank you to Philippa Wadsworth for all your time and advice, and to Alexandra Wilby, Judith Arkle and Claire Reid for kindly allowing me to adapt your recipes.

Thank you to all my family for your support and encouragement. Particular thanks to Claire Crook for all your help testing recipes, and to Louise Martin for being there from day one. Thank you for all those long days spent in the kitchen and for keeping me smiling amidst the chaos. Special thanks to Jean Harker for your time, generosity, wisdom and advice. Thank you to my wonderful sister, Lucy, for absolutely everything. I know I ask you for a lot of help. Thanks too, to Andy for being awesome.

I couldn't do what I do now without the never-ending support and generosity of my parents. Although I am supposed to be grown up, I really could not manage without everything you do for me, so thank you. Finally, thank you to Tony, for everything.

Quercus Editions Ltd
55 Baker Street
7th Floor, South Block
London
W1U 8EW

First published in 2013

A catalogue record of this book is available from the British Library

ISBN 978 1 78206 010 9

Publishing Director: Jenny Heller
Project Editor: Ione Walder
Produced by: Harris + Wilson
Design and Layout: A-Side Studio
Food styling: Lincoln Jefferson

Printed and bound in China

10 9 8 7 6 5 4 3 2 1

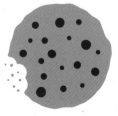